W9-ACW-071

Super STRING GAMES

by Camilla Gryski
Illustrated by Tom Sankey

Morrow Junior Books
New York

Text copyright © 1987 by Camilla Gryski
Illustrations copyright © 1987 by Tom Sankey
First published in Canada in 1987
by Kids Can Press, 585½ Bloor Street West,
Toronto, Ontario, CANADA M6G 1K5
Inquiries should be addressed to
William Morrow and Company, Inc.,
105 Madison Avenue, New York, NY 10016.
Printed in the United States of America.

1   2   3   4   5   6   7   8   9   10

Library of Congress Cataloging-in-Publication Data
Gryski, Camilla.
Super string games / by Camilla Gryski :
illustrated by Tom Sankey.
p.   cm.
Summary: Provides step-by-step instructions for creating twenty-
six string figures from around the world, including "The Fish Trap"
and "The Sea Snake."
ISBN 0-688-07684-X. ISBN 0-688-07685-8 (lib. bdg.)
1. String figures—Juvenile literature. [1. String figures.]
I. Sankey, Tom, ill.   II. Title.
GV1218.S8G79 1988
793.9—dc19   87-18365

For Honor Maude with thanks, and for my father,
Denis Milton, with love.

Table of Contents

Introduction

Super String Games is the third book of string games in a series. Like the games in the other two books, *Cat's Cradle, Owl's Eyes: A Book of String Games* and *Many Stars and More String Games*, the figures were collected by anthropologists from native peoples all over the world, and like those games, all the patterns are woven on your fingers with a loop of string. You can take a tour around the world with your fingers and your string, from the Arctic to the South Pacific, from North America to Asia and back again, as quickly as you can turn the pages of the book. You can create intricate symmetrical designs learned from the net makers of the South Pacific, and graphic string pictures collected from the Inuit string artists of the Arctic.

But super, wonderful string games are harder to learn than easy string games. It takes more words and pictures to tell you how to do them and so, before you begin, here's some practical advice and some encouragement.

One of the obvious difficulties you will face is how to turn the pages of the book when your hands are all tied up with string. I am sure that noses and toes have been used in the past, but here's an easy way to do it.

Turn your hands so that the palms are facing you, then close your middle, ring, and little fingers down over all the strings. Your index fingers and thumbs are free to turn the pages or write notes to yourself, and once you are holding onto the strings of the figure tightly, you can change the position of your hands without losing any loops.

It is also useful to hold down the upper corners of the pages with paperweights or rocks, especially if you are outside.

The more steps a figure has, the more patience you will need to learn it, but you will be amazed at how easily your fingers remember the steps — they will flow through 20 moves as easily as 10. But I wish I could be there to cheer you on around step 15 or 16 when the going gets a bit rough.

As you work through the book, you will notice that you sometimes need a longer string than usual. A middle length string is about 2.6 metres or 8½ feet. A long string is 3.4 metres or 11 feet.

You will also notice some new groups of moves that have names. Watch out for the Murray Opening, the Caroline Islands Extension, and an Inuit move, to Katilluik.

Since part of the charm of string games is the magical way they dissolve back into a loop of string, I've included ways to take apart certain figures without tangling.

And now a last word on string doodling. As I was doing the research for this book, I was struck by the number of figures that are variations on other figures and figures that build on other patterns, as if string artists were always looking for ways to extend the flow of movement and story. Perhaps these figures were created by accident as the artist tried to remember a figure, or perhaps the process was more deliberate; but string doodling, just letting your fingers vary the vocabulary they know — picking up and dropping loops, navahoing, then extending the figure in different ways — can be lots of fun. And if you manage to invent a spectacular string game, be sure to write it down. Every string artist has a figure that got away!

About the String

The Inuit used sinew or a leather thong to make their string figures. Other peoples farther south made twine from the inside of bark. We are told that Tikopian children in the Pacific Islands area preferred fibre from the hibiscus tree, although they would use a length of fishing line if it was handy. Some people even used human hair, finely braided.

Fortunately, you don't have to go out into the woods or cut your hair to get a good string for making string figures.

You can use ordinary white butcher's string knotted together at the ends. Macrame cord also works quite well, as it is thicker than string. A thicker string loop will better show off your string figures.

Dressmaker's supply stores sell nylon cord, (usually by the metre or foot). This kind of cord is probably the best, and because it is woven, not plied or twisted, it won't crease. It can be joined without a knot. A knot in your string loop can cause tangles, and figures that move won't go smoothly if there is a knot in the way.

How to Make Your String

You need about two metres (six feet) of string or cord, so that your string loop will measure one metre (three feet) when it is joined. This is a standard size. If this length seems uncomfortably long, a shorter string is fine for most of the figures.

The string can be either tied or melted together.

To tie your string

You need a knot that won't slip, so a square knot is best.

1. Lay the right end of the string across the left end.

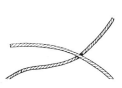

2. Put this right end under the left string to tie the first part of the knot.

3. Lay the new left end across the new right end.

4. Put this new left end under the new right string and tighten the knot.

5. Trim the ends to make the knot neat.

To melt your string

If the cord is nylon or some other synthetic fibre, you can melt the ends together. Joining the string takes practice, and it has to be done quickly while the cord is hot. You will probably need some help, so please do this with an adult.

1. Hold the ends of the string near each other, about one to two centimetres (one-half an inch) above a candle flame. If the ends are not melting at all, they are too far away from the flame. They will singe if you are holding them too close.

2. When the ends are gooey, stick them together.

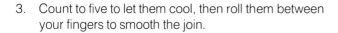

3. Count to five to let them cool, then roll them between your fingers to smooth the join.

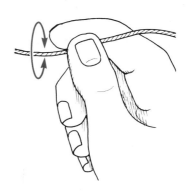

You have now made your "play string" or "ayahaak" as the Inuit call it.

Terminology
There's a Special Language

A long time ago, people made lists of the names of string figures, or brought back drawings of the finished patterns. Some even kept the string pattern itself, fastened to a piece of paper.

But once a string figure is finished, it is almost impossible to tell just how it was made. We can learn and teach each other string figures today because, in 1898, two anthropologists, Dr. A.C. Haddon and Dr. W.H.R. Rivers, invented a special language to describe the way string figures are made. Haddon and Rivers developed their special language to record all the steps it took to make the string figures they learned in the Torres Straits. Then, other anthropologists used this same language, or a simpler version of it, when they wanted to remember the string figures they saw in their travels.

The language used in this book to describe the making of the figures is similar to that used by Haddon and Rivers. The loops and the strings have names, and there are also names for some of the basic positions and moves.

About Loops

When the string goes around your finger or thumb, it makes a **loop.**

The loops take their names from their location on your hands: **thumb loop, index loop, middle finger loop, ring finger loop, little finger loop.**

If you move a loop from one finger to another, it gets a new name: a loop that was on your thumb but is now on your little finger is a new little finger loop.

Each loop has a **near string** — the one nearer (or closer) to you — and a **far string** — the one farther from you.

If there are two loops on your thumb or finger, one is the **lower loop** — the one near the base of your thumb or finger — and the other is the **upper loop** — the one near the top of your thumb or finger. Don't get these loops mixed up, and be sure to keep them apart.

About Making the Figures

As you make the figures in this book, you will be weaving the strings of the loops on your fingers. Your fingers or thumbs can go over or under the strings to pick up one or more strings, then go back to the basic position.

Sometimes you may **drop** or **release** a loop from your fingers.

It takes a little while to get used to holding your hands so that the strings don't drop off your fingers. If you accidentally drop a loop or a string, it is best to start all over again.

Now go and get your string — let's begin!

Names of the Strings

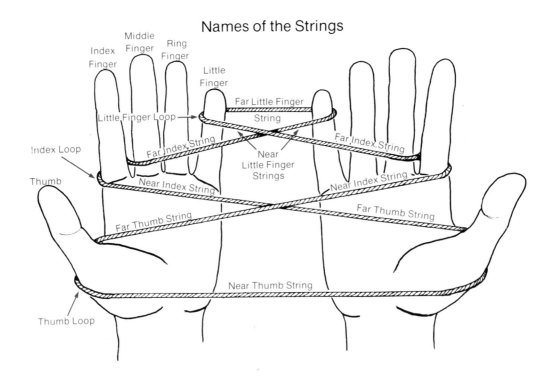

The Basic Position

Your hands begin in the **basic position** for most string figures and usually return to the basic position after each move.

1. Your hands are parallel, the palms are facing each other, and your fingers are pointing up.

The hands in some of the pictures are not in the basic position. The hands are shown with the palms facing you so that you can see all the strings clearly.

Position 1

1. With your hands in the basic position, hang the loop of string on your thumbs. Stretch your hands as far apart as you can to make the string loop tight.

2. Pick up the far thumb string with your little fingers. The string that goes across the palm of your hand is called the **palmar string.**

Opening A

Many string figures begin with **Opening A.**

1. Put the string loop on your fingers in Position 1.

2. With your right index finger, pick up from below the palmar string on your left hand, and return to the basic position pulling this string on the back of your index finger as far as it will go.

3. With your left index finger, pick up the right palmar string, from below, in between the strings of the loop that goes around your right index finger. Return to the basic position, again pulling out the palmar string as far as it will go.

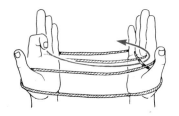
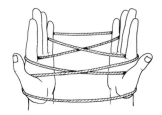

To Navaho a Loop

When you have two loops on your thumb or finger, a lower loop and an upper loop, you **Navaho** these loops by lifting the lower loop — with the thumb and index finger of your opposite hand, or with your teeth — up over the upper loop and over the tip of your finger or thumb.

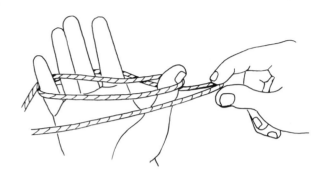

You can also Navaho a loop by tipping down your thumb or finger, letting the lower loop slip off, then straightening up your thumb or finger again.

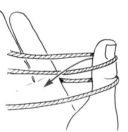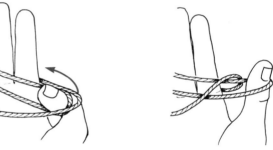

To Share a Loop

Sometimes you will **share a loop** between two fingers or a finger and your thumb. You use your opposite index finger and thumb to pull out the loop so that the other finger or thumb will fit into the loop as well.

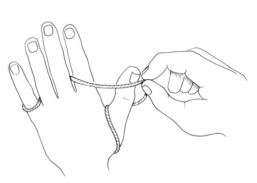

To Extend a Figure

Sometimes the strings may be woven and a figure may be finished, but it needs to be **extended** by pulling the hands apart, or by turning or twisting the hands in a certain way. Extending the figure makes a tangle of strings magically turn into a beautiful pattern.

To Take the Figure Apart

Always take the figures apart gently, as tugging creates knots. If the figure has top and bottom straight strings which frame the pattern, pull these apart and the pattern will dissolve.

Getting a String or Strings

When the instructions tell you to **get** a string or strings, your finger or thumb goes under that string, picks up that string on its back (the back of your finger or thumb is the side with the fingernail), then returns to the basic position carrying the string with it. The instructions will tell you if you are to use your fingers or thumb to pick up the strings in a different way.

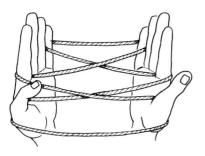 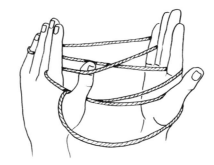 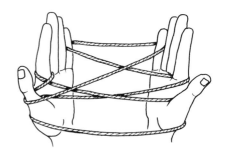

How to Double a String

For some figures, you can use a short string loop, or you can double your long string.

1. Hang the string loop over the fingers, but not the thumb, of your hand.

2. Wrap the back string of the hanging loop once around your hand.

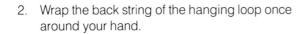

3. Take hold of everything that crosses the palm of your hand (the loop and one hanging string) and pull these strings out as far as they will go.

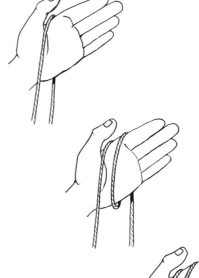

The Fish Trap

This Fish Trap, or Mashowo, was collected in South America by a zoologist named Lutz. He learned it from a twelve-year-old boy nicknamed Crickety who was a champion string figure artist.

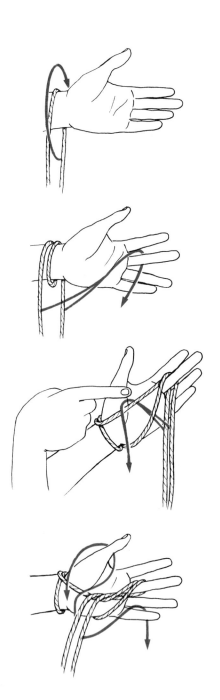

1. Put the string loop around your left wrist. There is a near wrist string and a far wrist string.

2. Your right index finger and thumb take the far wrist string and wrap it once around your left wrist.

3. Your right index finger and thumb take the long strings of the hanging loop and wrap them around your left middle finger. The strings go away from you between your left index finger and middle finger, around the back of your left middle finger, then come back towards you between your left middle finger and ring finger. Two strings cross your palm as they run up to your left middle finger.

4. Your right index finger goes, from the thumb side, under these two strings. Use this finger like a hook to get the strings of the long hanging loop. Bring the whole hanging loop back through under the palm strings. The strings of the long loop now hang down across your palm.

5. Your right index finger and thumb take the string of the long loop which is nearest to your left little finger and put it around the back of your left little finger.

6. Your right index finger and thumb take the hanging string nearest to your left thumb and put it around the back of your left thumb.

7. Your right index finger goes, from below, up under the string which crosses the base of your left index finger, and . . .

8. Your right middle finger goes, from below, up under the string which crosses the base of your left ring finger. Return your hands to the basic position.

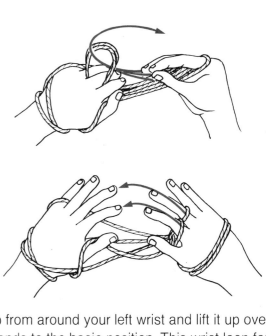

9. There is a double string loop around your left middle finger. Turn your left hand palm down and, from the back, with your right thumb and index finger pull out this double loop as far as you can. Let go of this loop.

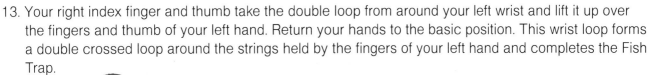

10. Now put your whole right hand through this double loop. Take your left middle finger out of its loop as you return your hands to the basic position. Your right hand now has a double wrist loop as well as an index loop and a middle finger loop.

11. Put your index fingers tip to tip. Slide the right index loop onto your left index finger.

12. Put your middle fingers tip to tip. Slide the right middle finger loop onto your left middle finger.

13. Your right index finger and thumb take the double loop from around your left wrist and lift it up over the fingers and thumb of your left hand. Return your hands to the basic position. This wrist loop forms a double crossed loop around the strings held by the fingers of your left hand and completes the Fish Trap.

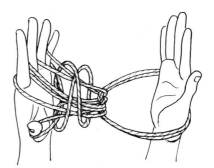

To take apart the Fish Trap, release the loops from the fingers of your left hand. Now take the loop off your right wrist and gently pull the old right wrist loops until the figure disappears.

The House of a Chief

This figure from the Hawaiian island of Oahu shows the house of a chief in the middle flanked by guards, the diamonds on each side of the house. It's a variation of the Fishnet, or Four Eyes, as it's called in Hawaii.

1. Do Opening A.

2. Your thumbs drop their loops.

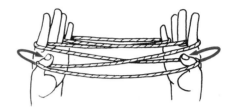

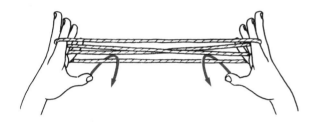

3. Turn your hands away from you with the palms facing out and the thumbs pointing down.

4. Your thumbs pick up, from below, the far little finger string (the bottom string) and return under the strings of the index loops. Your hands have returned to the basic position.

5. Your thumbs go over both strings of the index loops to get the near little finger strings and return.

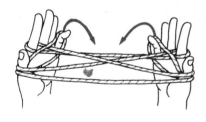

6. Your little fingers drop their loops. Each little finger can push off the opposite little finger loop.

On each hand there is a loop of string which runs around the index loop. These are the old little finger loops. When you hold your hands with the fingers pointing away from you, each of these loops has a top string and a bottom string.

7. With your right thumb and index finger, take hold of the bottom string of the old little finger loop on your left hand, pick it up and put it on your left little finger.

8. With your left thumb and index finger, pick up the bottom string of the old little finger loop on your right hand and put it on your right little finger. Return your hands to the basic position.

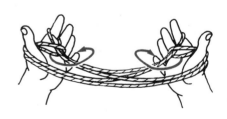

9. Your thumbs drop both their loops.

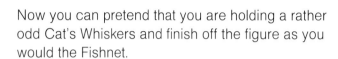

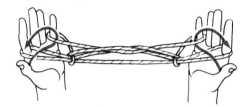

Now you can pretend that you are holding a rather odd Cat's Whiskers and finish off the figure as you would the Fishnet.

10. Your thumbs go over both strings of the index loops to get the near little finger strings and return.

11. Use your right thumb and index finger to pull out the left index loop and share it with your left thumb.

12. Use your left thumb and index finger to share the right index loop with your right thumb.

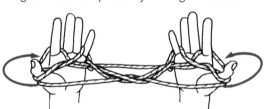

13. Navaho the thumb loops. You can tip down your thumbs to do this, or use your fingers or teeth.

14. Near each thumb there is a small string triangle. Your index fingers tip down to go from above into these triangles.

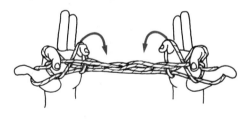

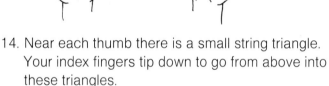

15. Gently take your little fingers out of their loops.

16. Turn your hands so that the palms are facing away from you. Don't worry about the index loops. They will just slip off your index fingers.

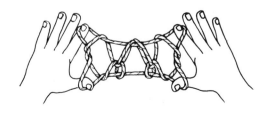

17. Your index fingers straighten up to extend the House of the Hawaiian Chief.

Collected by Lyle A. Dickey

The Lizard

The Lizard is a string trick that was first collected from the Torres Straits in the South Pacific. When you've learned it, you can dazzle your friends by doing it several times in a row. In the Loyalty Islands, this slippery string trick was used when it was time to stop playing with string.

1. Hold the string loop with your left hand. Let the long loop hang down freely.
   The loop has a near side (close to you), and a far side (far from you on the other side of the strings).

2. Hold your right hand palm down with the fingers facing away from you, and put your hand through the string loop from the near side.

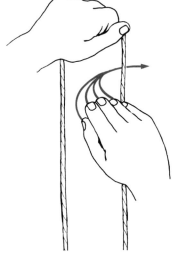

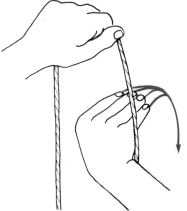

3. Tilt your right hand until the thumb faces down and then bend your wrist until your fingers are facing towards the right. The right hanging string is caught in the crook of your wrist.

4. Catch this string (the right hanging string) on the back of your right thumb, then let this string slide over the rest of the fingers of your right hand until it is looped around your right wrist. Your right hand rotates as you do this, the fingers facing down, then towards the left. Your palm is facing in.

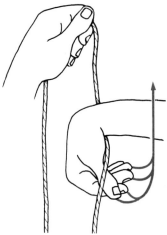

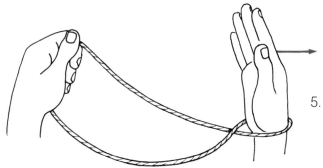

5. Continue to rotate your right hand until your fingers are facing up. Now turn your hand so that the palm is facing out, away from you. The right string of the hanging loop is still around your wrist.

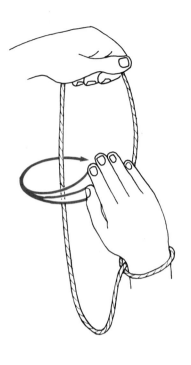

6. Move your right hand, palm out, across the front of the figure to the left of the left string of the hanging loop, then away from you to the far side of the string loop.

7. Move your hand, still palm out, a little to the right, until it is behind the hanging loop.
Your right hand has taken the right string of the hanging loop with it. This right string crosses over the left string, creating an upper space framed by the strings of the loop.

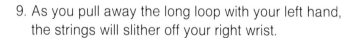

8. Bring your right hand, back first, towards you between the strings of this small upper space.

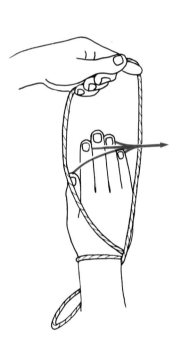

9. As you pull away the long loop with your left hand, the strings will slither off your right wrist.

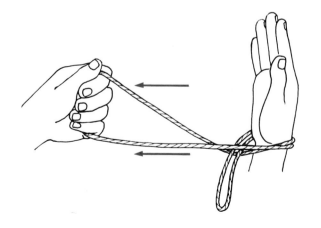

Now do it again!

Collected by M.D. Rivers and A.C. Haddon

17

The Parakeets' Playground

This string figure sequence from Fiji begins with the Parakeets' Playground. You can go on to make the Parakeet's Home, then finish up with a wonderfully realistic turtle.

If you would like a friend to play, you can stop along the way to make the Sova, or Long-handled Basket.

The same figures tell the story of some crabs who ran away and, finally, if you're having a wonderful time, you can make the Elastic Band which can stretch and shrink forever.

1. Do Position 1.

2. Put your whole right hand, thumb too, under the left palmar string and, as you pull it out, let the string loop slide down around your right wrist.

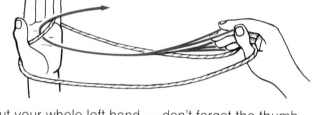

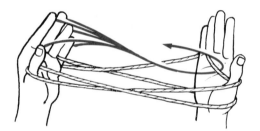

3. Put your whole left hand — don't forget the thumb — under the right palmar string and, as you pull it out, let the string loop slide down around your left wrist.

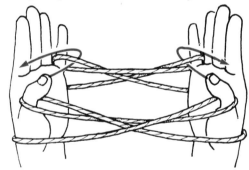

4. Your thumbs get the near little finger strings and return.

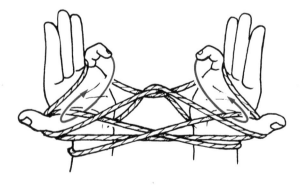

5. Your little fingers get the far thumb strings and return.

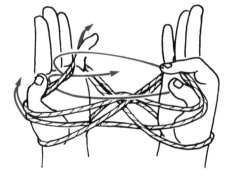

6. Each hand now has double palmar strings. Your right thumb and index finger take hold of the double left palmar strings and take them off your left thumb and little finger. Continue to hold them while you . . .

7. Begin to take your left hand out of its wrist loop and, as the wrist loop slides off, grab it with your left thumb and index finger.

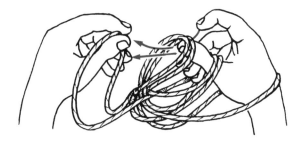

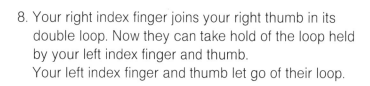

8. Your right index finger joins your right thumb in its double loop. Now they can take hold of the loop held by your left index finger and thumb.
Your left index finger and thumb let go of their loop.

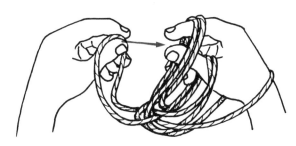

9. Your left thumb and little finger go, from the top, down into the double shared right thumb/index loop. They return with this loop in Position 1 on your left hand.

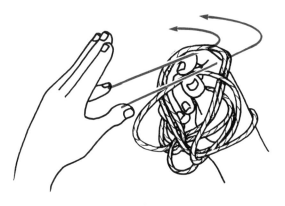

10. Your right thumb and index finger put the loop they are holding onto your left index finger. Make sure there is no twist in the left index loop. The strings should run straight down to the centre of the figure.

Now you must repeat this process for your right hand.

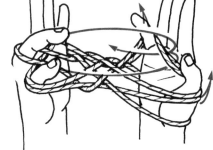

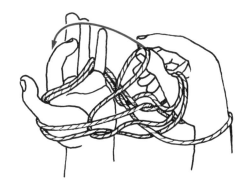

11. Your left thumb and index finger, without losing their loops, take the double palmar strings off your right thumb and little finger. Continue to hold them while you . . .

Keep going...

12. Begin to take your right hand out of its wrist loop and, as the wrist loop slides off, grab it with your right thumb and index finger.

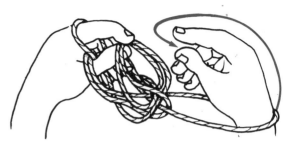

13. Your left index finger joins your left thumb in its double loop. Now they can take hold of the loop held by your right index finger and thumb. Your right index finger and thumb let go of their loop.

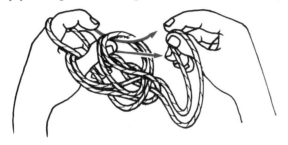

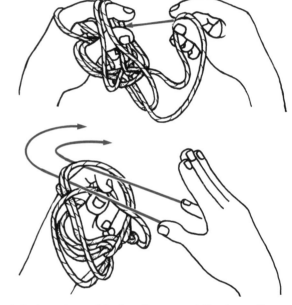

14. Your right thumb and little finger go, from the top, down into the double left shared thumb/index loop. They take it off your left thumb and index finger and return with it in Position 1 on your right hand.

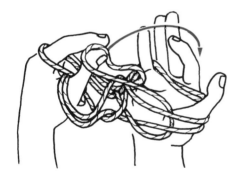

This is the Parakeets' Playground, a place where the branches of the trees are interlaced like the strings in the pattern.

15. Your left thumb and index finger put the loop they are holding onto your right index finger. Make sure that there is no twist in the right index loop.

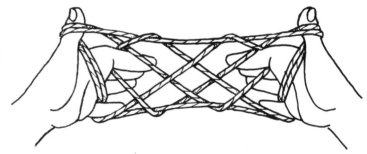

To best display the figure, turn your hands so that the fingers are facing away from you. Now tip your index fingers towards each other to widen the central interlacing string pattern.

If you want to have a friend help you to make a basket with two long handles, you can interrupt the sequence here. If not, skip over to the Home of the Parakeet.

The Basket

1. Your friend must hook his/her index finger, from below, over all the strings which criss-cross in the centre of the figure. So, his/her index finger goes, from below, up into the right index loop, across the strings, then down into the left index loop.

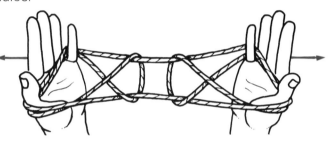

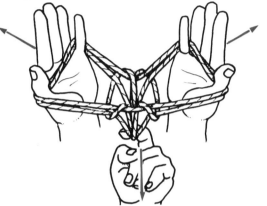

2. Your index fingers drop their loops. As your friend pulls down on the strings, you pull up on the handles. This is the Sova, the basket with long handles.

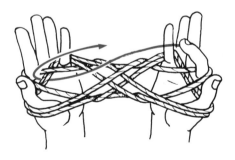

3. When your friend lets go of the loops s/he is holding and you pull your hands apart, you make the figure of Koro and Wakaia, two islands which face each other across a channel.

The Home of the Parakeet

To make the Home of the Parakeet, the shady forest glade surrounded by trees, first make the Parakeets' Playground.

1. Return your hands to the basic position.

2. Your right index finger, without losing its loop, goes through the left index loop to get the left double palmar strings (as in Opening A) and returns.

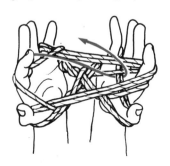

3. Your left index finger goes through both sets of right index loops to get the double right palmar strings and returns.

Keep going...

4. Each index finger has two sets of loops: a lower single loop and upper double loops. Use your teeth or fingers to Navaho the index loops. In each case, the lower single loop goes up over the upper double loops and up over the top of the index finger.

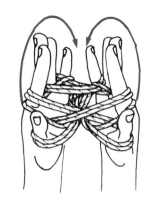

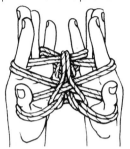

This is the parakeet's home.

The Turtle

Now to make the wonderful turtle, first make the Home of the Parakeet.

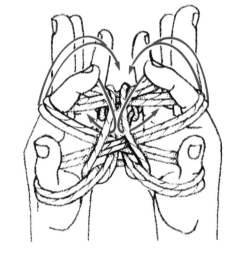

1. There are two straight strings which run from front to back across the figure. (They are the Navahoed lower index loops.) Each index finger hooks down over the straight string nearest to it. It catches the straight string and carries it back through its own index loops. Don't worry about the original double index loops. They will just slide off your index fingers.
   Give each new index loop, held in the hooks of your index fingers, a little tug to tighten the turtle's head and tail.

   Now you can lay the turtle across the palm of your left hand. Your right hand drops all its loops. Take your left index finger out of its loop as well. If you like, you can gently lift the turtle off your fingers and put it down on a flat surface. The turtle will walk along if you use your thumbs and index fingers to move its leg loops.

This string sequence tells a different story when you use the names given to the figures in the Loyalty Islands.

In the Parakeets' Playground figure, the strings now represent the paths among the rocks for little crabs.

The parakeet's home becomes a hole for crabs.

To show the crabs running off into their holes, make the Turtle, then release the loops from your index fingers and pull your hands apart. Two loops disentangle themselves and skitter off in opposite directions.

The Elastic Band

If you are having so much fun with this sequence of figures that you don't want it to end, here's a way that you can catch the crabs as they are running away and turn them into the Elastic Band. This ending comes from Japan.

1. Let the crabs run away a little. Now return your hands to the basic position and look down at the figure from the top. The figure is made up of two string X's. The X strings then loop around the framing strings.

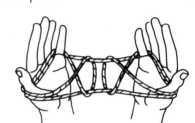

2. Your index fingers and middle fingers tip down to pinch the strings of the X's where they cross in the middle.

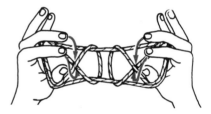

3. Now your index fingers and middle fingers come up from below through the triangles made by the strings of the X's as they loop around the framing strings.

4. Your index fingers and middle fingers straighten up, carrying the strings of the X's on their backs.
To make the elastic band stretch, let your fingers collapse and then pull your hands apart.
To make the elastic band shrink, stretch your fingers apart and your hands will move closer together.

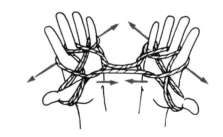

P.S. You can take a shortcut to the Elastic Band. Just make the Parakeets' Playground and drop the loops from your index fingers. Pull your hands apart a little and you're all set.

Collected by James Hornell

23

The Sea Snake

This Sea Snake comes from the Torres Straits in the South Pacific. It slithers away and disappears right before your eyes. Now you see it, now you don't!

1. Do Opening A.

2. Turn your left hand so that the palm is facing away from you. Your left thumb presses down on all the strings, then comes towards you under all the strings. Your whole hand follows your thumb underneath all the strings and up until it returns to the basic position. All the strings are wrapped around the back of your left hand.

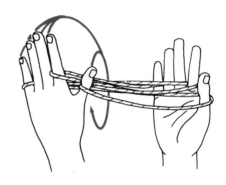

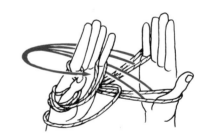

3. Put the tips of the fingers and thumb of your left hand together. Your whole left hand goes, from the top, down into the right index loop. Take your right index finger out of its loop as you do this. The right index loop is now around your left wrist.

4. Now unwind the strings from around your left hand. Your left hand should be back where it started. Your left hand has a thumb loop, an index loop, a little finger loop, and a wrist loop.

5. Your left index finger drops its loop. Now pull the strings apart as far as they will go.

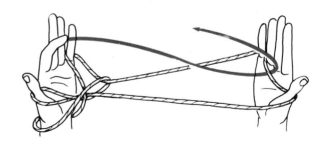

6. Your left index finger picks up, from below, the right palmar string and returns.

7. Your right index finger and thumb take hold of the loop around your left wrist. They lift this loop up over the fingers and thumb of your left hand and let it lie around the strings which cross from hand to hand. Return your hands to the basic position.

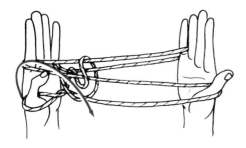

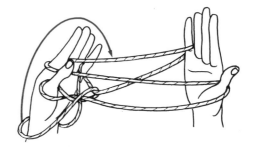

8. Your left thumb drops its loop.

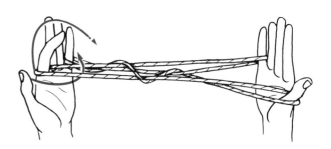

9. Your left thumb goes, from below, up into the left index loop. Your left index finger drops its loop. You have transferred the left index loop to your left thumb.

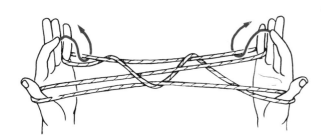

10. Your index fingers go, from above, down into the little finger loops. They pick up, on their backs, the far little finger string and return. Keep this string high up on your index fingers and press your index fingers and middle fingers together to steady the top framing string of the figure.

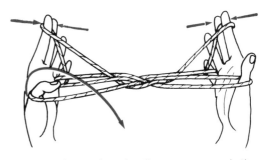

11. Your left thumb drops its loop — the rounded tail of the Sea Snake.

12. Turn your hands so that the fingers are pointing away from you. When your right thumb gently pulls on its loop, the Sea Snake will appear. Remember to keep the top framing string, held between your index and middle fingers, steady while you extend the snake.

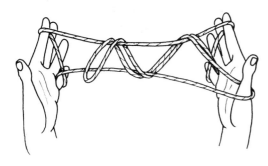

To make the snake slither off to the right, pull your hands apart and let the strings slide through the fingers of your right hand.

Collected by M.D. Rivers and A.C. Haddon

The Looper Caterpillar

This delightful moving figure from the South Pacific has many names. In New Caledonia, it's called the Looper Caterpillar. You can see why as you make it loop along. In the Solomon Islands, it's known as Worm Creeping. The Nauruans named it the Dancer, and in the Caroline Islands it's One Chief. An easy way of making it was collected in Papua New Guinea. There it's called Zissoci (Scissors?), and you are supposed to put the figure up to someone's head and pretend to cut the hair.

1. Do Position 1.

2. Your right thumb and index finger take the near left thumb string and wrap it once around your left thumb.

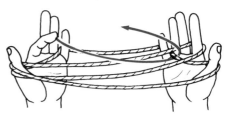

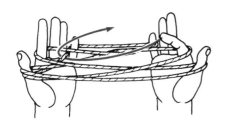

3. Your right index finger goes, from below, up into this new little left thumb loop and returns.

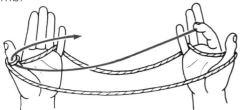

4. Your left index finger gets the right palmar string, as in Opening A, and returns.

5. Your right index finger gets the left palmar string, as in Opening A, and returns. Your right index finger now has two loops — an upper loop and a lower loop. Be sure to keep them apart and don't let them get mixed up.

6. Turn your hands so that your right palm is facing down and the fingers of your right hand are pointing to the left.

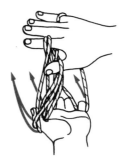

7. Your left hand drops all its loops.

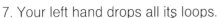

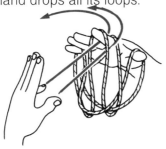

8. Your left thumb and little finger go into the upper right index loop. They take this loop off your right index finger. The string is in Position 1 on your left hand and your left hand is now in the basic position. Don't return your right hand to the basic position yet.

9. Put your left thumb and your right index finger tip to tip. Now slide the remaining right index loop onto your left thumb and return your hands to the basic position.

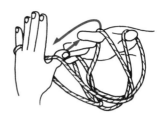

10. Your left thumb and index finger, without losing any loops, take hold of the right far thumb string and the right near little finger string. Take your right thumb out of its loop and put it back into its loop from the top.

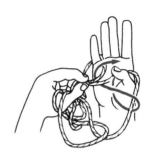

11. Your right thumb also goes, from below, up into the right little finger loop and returns carrying the near little finger string as well as its own loop.
Your left index finger and thumb drop the strings they are holding and return to the basic position.

The figure is extended using the Caroline Extension:

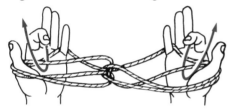

13. Your thumbs press against the strings which run from your index fingers down to your thumbs. Keep each index finger and thumb, with the string between them, pressed tightly together. Don't let this string move at all.

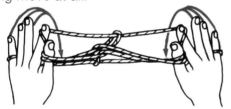

12. Turn your hands until the palms are facing up. Your index fingers tip down over the palmar strings to go, from below, up into the thumb loops. They get the far thumb strings and return. Keep these strings high up on your index fingers.

14. To extend the Caterpillar, turn your hands so that the palms are facing out. Curl your middle, ring, and little fingers down over the far little finger string. This is comfortable and helps to steady the bottom framing string as the caterpillar walks along.

To make the Caterpillar walk, you alternately extend and collapse the figure.

To collapse the figure, rotate your hands until the palms are facing each other.

To extend the figure again, rotate your hands until the palms are facing out.

Now your Caterpillar can crawl along your lap or up somebody's arm.

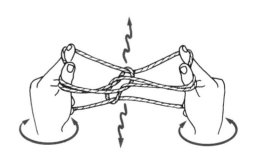

Collected by Philip Noble

The Caribou

The Inuit made many string figures of the animals they hunted. In some parts of the Arctic, this one is called the Caribou. The caribou's antler can also be seen as a big ear, so it's called the Rabbit as well.

1. Do Opening A.

2. Turn your right hand so that the palm is facing away from you and hook your right index finger down over both strings of the right little finger loop. Let the right index loop slip down until it too is held in the hook of your right index finger. Don't drop the right thumb loop as you do this!

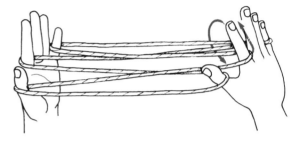

3. Now turn your right hand back until the palm is facing you. Your right index finger carries its strings with it as it moves towards you.

4. Your right index finger goes, from below, up into the right thumb loop. It hooks down over the near right thumb string. Now turn your right hand until the palm is facing away from you. As you straighten up your right index finger, the near right thumb string will curve around it to become a new right index loop. Return your hands to the basic position.

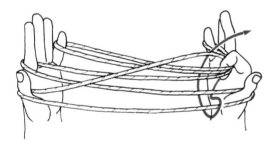

5. Your right thumb drops its loop.

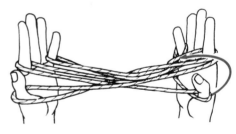

6. Your right index finger now has two loops. To put a twist in these loops, rotate your index finger away from you, down, towards you, and up. Don't drop the little finger loop as you do this!

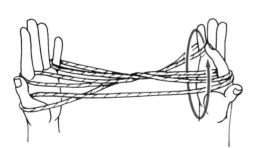

7. Put your right thumb, from below, up into the twisted right index loops. Your right thumb and index finger share the right index loops.

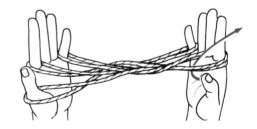

8. Now your right thumb and index finger take hold of the near left index string and take the loop right off your left index finger.

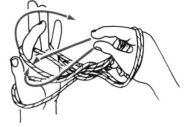

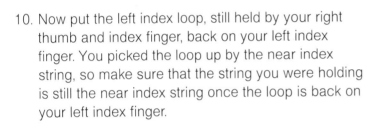

9. Your left thumb and index finger take the loops right off your right index finger and thumb. These loops go over the loop held by your right index finger and thumb. Drop these old right thumb/index loops in the middle of the figure.

10. Now put the left index loop, still held by your right thumb and index finger, back on your left index finger. You picked the loop up by the near index string, so make sure that the string you were holding is still the near index string once the loop is back on your left index finger.

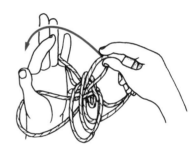

11. Your left thumb drops its loop.

12. Turn your hands so that the fingers are pointing away from you and pull your hands gently apart to extend the figure. The Caribou is represented by an antler, a face, and a looped body which curves around the strings.

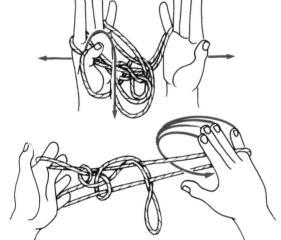

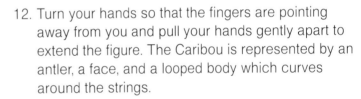

13. Put the fingers of your right hand, from above, down into the right little finger loop. Your right little finger joins the other fingers of your right hand in their loop.

You may have to use your thumb to untangle the Caribou's antler, face, and body.

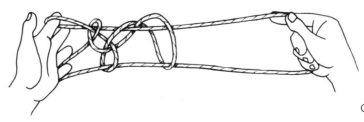

Collected by Dr. G.B. Gordon

The Setting Sun

This string figure was collected in the Torres Straits in 1898. When you have made the sun, you can make it disappear into the sea, leaving only the line of the horizon. Use your middle length string for this figure.

1. Do Opening A.

2. Turn your hands so that the palms are facing you. Your little fingers come towards you across the strings to get the near thumb string and return.

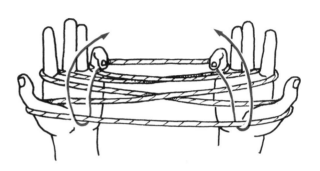

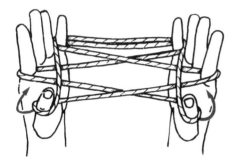

3. Your thumbs drop their loops.

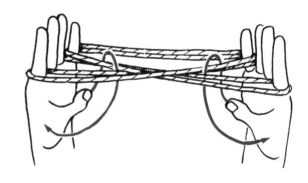

4. Your thumbs go under the strings of the index loops to get the double near little finger strings. They return under the index loops.

5. Your little fingers drop their loops.

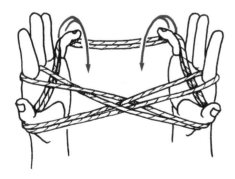

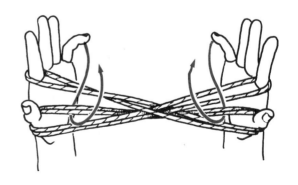

6. Your little fingers come towards you over the strings of the index loops to get the double far thumb strings and return.

30

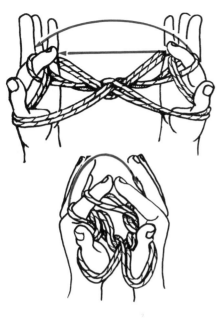

7. Your index fingers are going to trade their loops.

   Put your index fingers tip to tip.

   Slide the right index loop over onto your left index finger.

   Your right thumb and index finger pick up the lower left index loop (the original left index loop). They lift it over the upper left index loop and off your left index finger.

   Steady this loop with the fingers of your left hand while your right index finger goes, from below, up into its new loop.

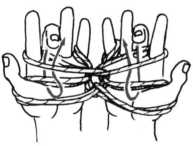

8. Your middle fingers tip down into the index loops. Then they go, from below, up into the thumb loops to get the double far thumb strings. They return carrying these strings back through the index loops.

   This is a tricky move, so you may have to use some of your other fingers to help get the middle finger loops back through the index loops.

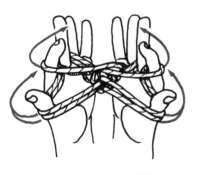

9. Your thumbs and your index fingers drop their loops.

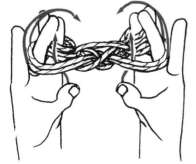

10. Your thumbs go, from below, up into the middle finger loops. Your middle fingers drop their loops. You've transferred the middle finger loops to your thumbs.

Keep going...

11. Look at the string figure from the top. It should look like two eyes, with a double string cross in the middle. You may have to push the double strings which run across the figure from side to side out of the way so you can see the X more clearly. Now your index fingers tip down into the eye spaces of the figure. They catch on their backs the top strings of the X and return. (If you are trying to do this figure with a regular length string, it will be impossibly awkward from now on.)

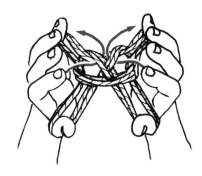

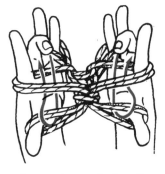

12. Once again, your middle fingers tip down into the index loops. This time they are double index loops. Your middle fingers go, from below, up into the thumb loops to get the double far thumb strings and return carrying these strings back through the index loops.

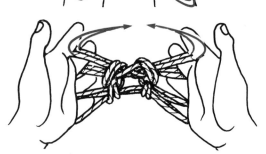

13. Your thumbs and your index fingers drop their double loops. Pull your hands apart a little to tighten these dropped loops.

Now you have made the sun with its rays — the four loops held on your fingers. To make the sun set, drop the loops from your middle fingers and pull out the little finger loops. The figure dissolves, leaving only the horizon.

If you would like your sun to have more rays, you can move one of the two loops on your left middle finger onto your left index finger. Then move one of the two loops on your right middle finger onto your right index finger. To make this sun set, you will have to drop both index and both middle finger loops before you pull out the little finger loops.

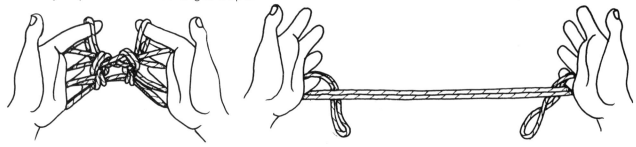

Collected by M.D. Rivers and A.C. Haddon

A Butterfly

This Navaho Indian string butterfly has a rolled up proboscis just like a real one. You can even flap the wings to make it fly.

The Butterfly begins with the Navaho Opening.

1. Hold the string loop with your hands about 10 cm (four inches) apart.

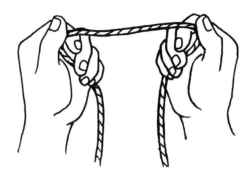

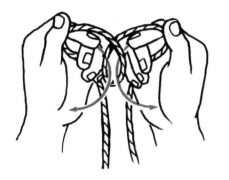

2. Make a small loop in the string you are holding.

3. Put your index fingers from behind into this string loop. Your index fingers are pointing towards you.

4. Turn your index fingers down, away from you, and up. The rest of your fingers are still holding on to the hanging strings of the big loop.

5. The strings you are holding with your hands cross in the middle to make an X. Your thumbs bring forward the bottom strings of the X and pull them out as far as they will go. As you pull out the thumb loops, your middle, ring, and little fingers let go of their strings.

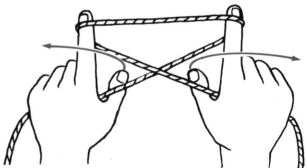

This is the Navaho Opening.

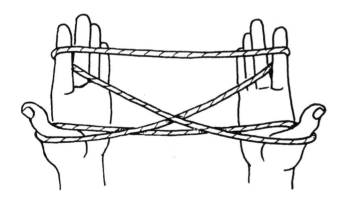

Keep going...

6. Now you are going to put five twists in each index loop. It is easier to do this if you keep the index loops high up on your index fingers. Twist the index loops by rotating both your index fingers away from you, down, towards you and up. Make sure that the twists are in the index loops and not around your index fingers. Repeat this four more times.

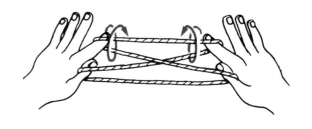

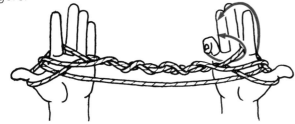

7. Your thumbs go, from below, up into the index loops and return. You've shared the index loops with your thumbs.

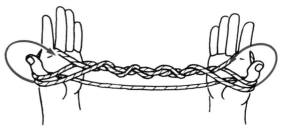

8. Navaho the thumb loops. Make sure that you Navaho the original lower thumb loop. It's easy to mix them up.

You have to rotate the figure before you can extend it, so you will have to shift the loops around on your fingers.

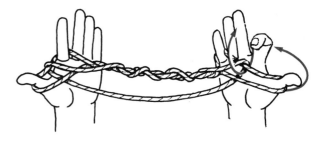

9. Your right little finger goes, from below, up into the right index loop. Your right index finger drops its loop.

10. Your right index finger tips down to go, from below, up into your right thumb loop. Your right thumb drops its loop.

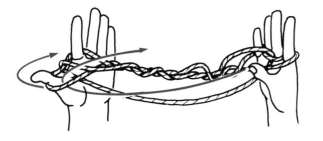

11. Your right thumb goes, from below, up into your left thumb loop. Your left thumb drops its loop.

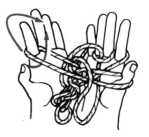

12. Your left thumb goes, from below, up into your left index loop. Your left index finger drops its loop.

13. Your left index finger goes, from below, up into your right little finger loop. Your right little finger drops its loop.

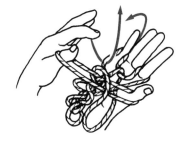

14. Turn your hands so that the fingers are pointing away from you and begin to pull your hands gently apart. As you do this, the strings which make up the butterfly's proboscis will roll up in the centre of the figure.

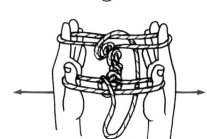

Don't pull your hands so far apart that you roll up the butterfly's wings as well. Leave some of the loop you are rolling up hanging below the strings of the figure.

15. To pull down the lower framing strings of the figure and extend the wings, your middle, ring, and little fingers go, from below, up into the index loops to join the index fingers. Now your middle, ring, and little fingers hook down and hold the near index strings *and* the far thumb strings.

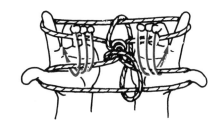

16. When you have extended the figure, you may have a snail instead of a butterfly, so use your teeth or a convenient finger to slide the wing loop from the right of the butterfly's proboscis to the left.

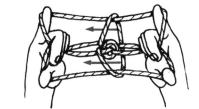

17. Keep the thumb loops and index loops high up on your thumbs and index fingers. Now flap the butterfly's wings by moving your thumbs and index fingers towards each other, then away from each other.

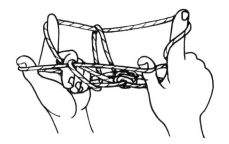

To disentangle this figure, drop all the loops except the left thumb loop. Now pull out this loop to make it bigger and the butterfly will unravel.

Collected by Caroline Furness Jayne

The Sardines

The Sardines is a fishy string tale which comes from the Loyalty Islands in the South Pacific. You can use your string to illustrate each step of the story as you tell it. Watch out for the surprise ending!

In the Solomon Islands, the same string sequence is called the Tide. The string pictures show the water at low and at high tide.

1. Hold the string loop with your hands about 10 cm (four inches) apart.

2. Make a small loop in the string you are holding.

3. Put your thumbs from the front into this small loop. Your thumbs are pointing away from you.

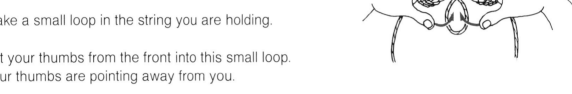

4. Your fingers let go of the long hanging strings of the figure. These hanging strings make a large loop.

5. Put your little fingers from the front into this large hanging loop and pull your hands apart as far as they will go. Return your hands to the basic position. The figure is extended using the Caroline Extension, steps 6, 7, and 8.

6. Turn your hands until the palms are facing up. Your index fingers tip down over the palmar strings. They go, from below, up into the thumb loops and return with the far thumb string.

7. Your thumbs press against the strings which run from your index fingers down to your thumbs. Keep each index finger and thumb, with the string between them, pressed tightly together. Don't let this string move at all.

8. Now turn your hands so that the palms are facing out. Keep your index fingers tall, but curl your middle, ring, and little fingers down over the far little finger string.

This is the low tide. So far there are no sardines.

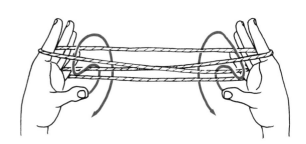

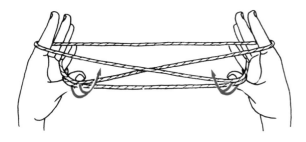

9. Turn your hands until the palms are facing each other and straighten up your middle, ring, and little fingers. Now take your thumbs right out of their loops.

10. Your thumbs go under the strings of the index loops and under the strings of the little finger loops. They get both strings of the little finger loops and begin to return.

11. Your thumbs go, from below, up into the index loops.

12. Hook your thumbs down over the far index string. Don't worry about the little finger strings. They will look after themselves.

13. Turn your hands until the palms are facing away from you and the thumbs are pointing down. Move your fingers sideways towards each other until your hands look exactly like the ones in the picture.

14. Catch the bottom string — the old far index string — on the backs of your thumbs and return your hands to the basic position.

15. Your index fingers drop their loops.

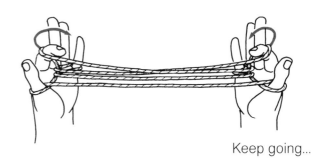

Keep going...

16. Your thumbs get the near little finger strings and return.

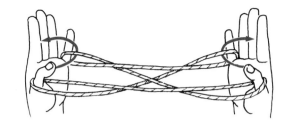

Do the Caroline Extension again to make some sardines.

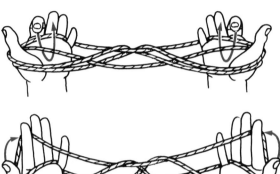

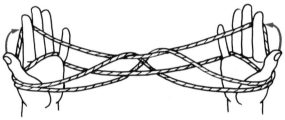

17. Repeat step 6.

18. Repeat step 7.

19. Repeat step 8.

This time, there are two sardines. In North Queensland, this step shows a Fish Hawk, wings spread wide.

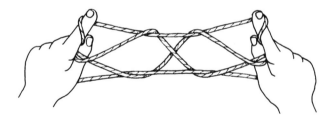

Now repeat steps 9-19 to make four sardines. The number of sardines increases by two each time you go through the sequence of moves. The longer the string, the more sardines you can make.

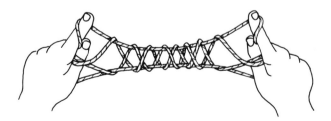

Many diamonds represent the high tide.

Here's the fishy story you can tell:

> A fisherman sees two sardines swimming by. He sees four sardines, six sardines, then eight sardines. (Eight is as many as can be done comfortably with a regular length string.)
>
> But before he can catch them, along come two big hungry fish.

To make the hungry fish:

Turn your hands so that the palms are facing each other.

Your thumbs drop both their loops.

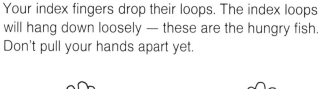

Your index fingers drop their loops. The index loops will hang down loosely — these are the hungry fish. Don't pull your hands apart yet.

Your thumbs get the near little finger strings. Turn your hands so that the fingers are pointing away from you.

Now pull your hands apart to unravel the figure and to show your audience how those hungry fish gobble up all the sardines. The fisherman, of course, is too late. By the time he gets there, all the sardines, and the hungry fish, are gone. The sea — your string loop — is empty.

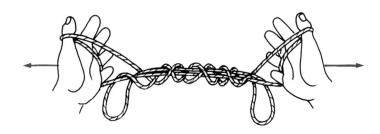

Collected by Honor Maude

39

The Taro Patch/Hawaiian Stars

This string game story sequence takes you from the water taro patch (taro is a food plant), to the sugar cane field. It shows you the swamp bird or Poule Sultane, then the bird caught in a trap. The Taro Patch comes from the Loyalty Islands in the South Pacific.

In Hawaii, this figure is called Po, or Night. You can see the Hawaiian sky at night, full of stars. There's a special chant to say while you make the stars disappear at dawn.

1. Do Opening A.

2. Your thumbs go under the strings of the index loops and under the near little finger strings to go, from below, up into the little finger loops.

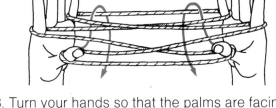

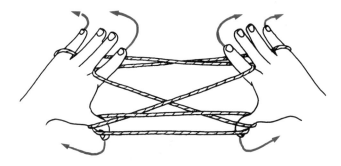

3. Turn your hands so that the palms are facing out and the thumbs are pointing down. Be careful not to lose the original thumb loops as you do all this. Move your fingers sideways towards each other until your hands look like the ones in the picture.

4. Catch the bottom string — the far little finger string — on the backs of your thumbs and return your hands to the basic position. Each thumb now has two loops.

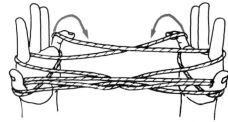

5. Your little fingers drop their loops.

6. Your middle, ring, and little fingers tip down to go, from below, up into the index loops. They hook down over and hold the near index strings.

7. Now you want to carry the double far thumb strings through the index loops. Your index fingers tip down to go, from above, into the thumb loops. They hook down over the double far thumb strings. Don't worry about the old index loops.

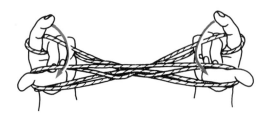

8. Turn your hands until the palms are facing out. As your index fingers straighten up, the double far thumb strings will curve around your index fingers to become new index loops. Return your hands to the basic position.

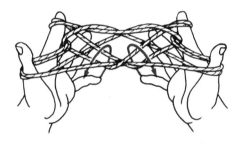

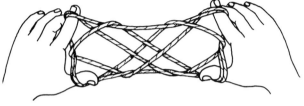

To make the Sugar Cane Field:

9. Your middle, ring, and little fingers drop their loops. This is the Taro Patch.

10. Turn your hands so that the fingers are pointing away from you and the palms are facing up. Your little fingers go, from below, up into the central diamond of the figure.

11. Each little finger hooks down over the two strings between it and the bottom framing string of the figure.

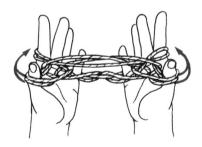

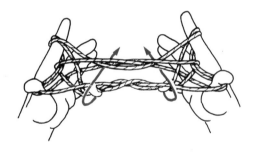

12. Now your little fingers come towards you to go under the straight near thumb string. They catch this string on their backs and return with it through the central diamond of the figure.

13. Your thumbs drop their double loops. You can use your opposite thumb to help push off the loops.

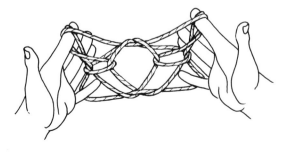

14. Extend the figure by pulling your hands apart a little and display it with your fingers pointing away from you.

Keep going...

To make the brightly colored Poule Sultane or swamp bird:

15. Each index finger has two loops. Your thumbs go up into the lower index loops from below. They catch on their backs the lower straight near index string.

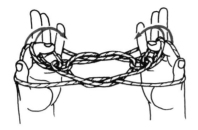

16. Your index fingers drop both their loops. You can use your middle fingers to push these loops off.

17. Make sure that your fingers are pointing away from you and begin to gently pull your hands apart until you can see what might be two eyes in the centre at the top of the figure. If you pull out too far, you will lose the eyes and end up with a knot.

The trap has been set. To trip it and catch the bird:

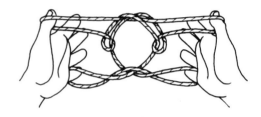

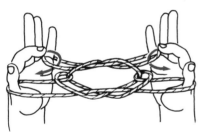

18. Return your hands to the basic position. Your index fingers tip down to go, from above, into the little finger loops. They hook down over the near little finger strings.

19. Turn your hands so that the palms are facing you. As you straighten up your index fingers, the near little finger strings will curve around them to become new index loops. Keep these index loops high up on your index fingers. Press your index fingers and middle fingers together to keep the loops steady.

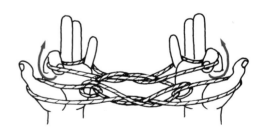

20. Turn your hands so that the fingers are once more pointing away from you.
Give the strings a little tug to tighten the figure. This will make sure that the trap really springs when it is tripped.

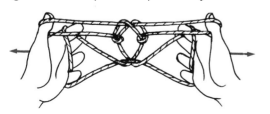

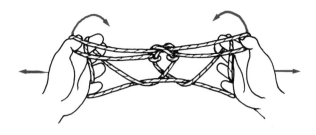

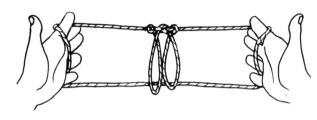

21. Your thumbs drop their loops.

22. Pull your hands apart slightly. The trap will be sprung as the framing strings of the figure untwist, and you will see the bird caught.

Now you can make up your own story to explain what the swamp bird was doing in the sugar cane field, who laid the trap, and how the bird got caught in it. What do you think happened when the bird was caught in the trap? Do you think he escaped?

You can use the same string figure to make the Hawaiian stars that disappear when the dawn comes.

Follow steps 1-9 to make the Hawaiian sky. As you extend the figure, seven diamond-shaped stars appear.

The chant goes like this:

At night, at night,
The stars overhang us.

Now to make the stars disappear as it gets light:

A straight string runs across each index loop. Your index fingers tip down, almost out of their loops. They catch on their backs the straight strings that cross their loops and return. It is easier to do this if you turn your hands so that the palms are facing you. The old index loops will slip off your index fingers to become far thumb strings again.

The stars have gone. Say:

At dawn
They are gone.

To make the stars appear again, just finish off the figure. You are at the end of step 5, so do steps 6-9 again.
You can make the stars appear and disappear as many times as you like.

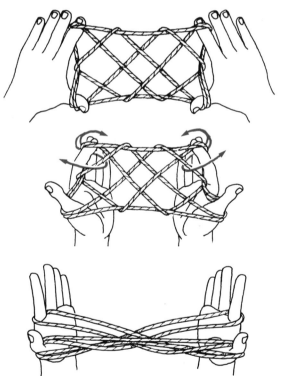

The Taro Patch collected by Honor Maude
Hawaiian Stars collected by Lyle A. Dickey

43

The Porcupine

The Porcupine is the Klamath Indian name for this figure, but the Inuit call it the Wolverine, the Wolf, or the Red Fox. Diamond Jenness collected a chant about a Red Fox and a place with no wind from the natives of Barrow in Alaska.

1. Do Opening A.

   Your index fingers exchange their loops.

2. Put your index fingers tip to tip. Slide the right index loop onto your left index finger.

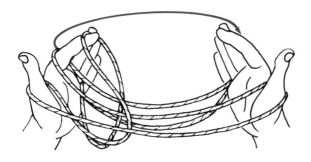

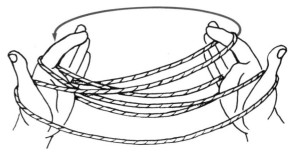

3. Your right thumb and index finger pick up the lower original left index loop and lift it up over the upper left index loop and right off your left index finger.

4. Your right index finger goes, from below, up into the loop held by your right thumb and index finger.

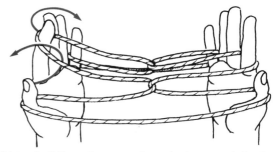

5. Your left thumb goes, from below, up into the left index loop.
   Your left index finger drops its loop.
   Be sure to keep the thumb loops apart and don't let them get mixed up.

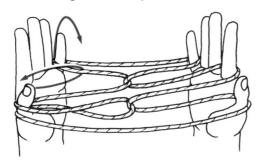

6. Your left thumb goes, from below, up into the left little finger loop. Your left little finger drops its loop. Your left thumb now has three loops! Don't let them get mixed up and be sure to keep them apart.

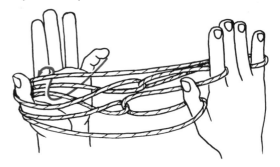

7. Your left little finger goes, from below, up into the left thumb loops. It pushes away, on its back, the two lower far thumb strings, then hooks down and holds the upper far thumb string.

8. Your left index finger and middle finger go down into the left thumb loops from above. Your left index finger comes out towards you between the middle and the lowest near thumb strings.

Your left middle finger comes out towards you under the lowest near thumb string.

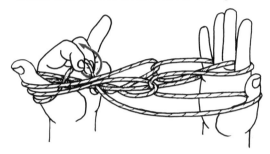

10. Your left thumb drops all its loops.

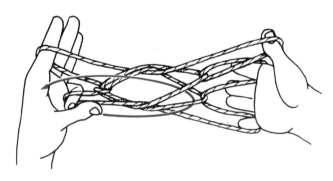

13. Your left thumb goes, from below, up into the left index loop and returns with the left near index string.

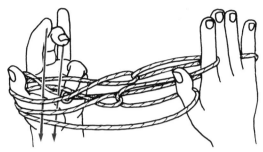

9. Pinch the lowest near thumb string between your left index finger and middle finger and turn your left hand until the palm is facing out. As you straighten up your index finger, the lowest near thumb string will curve around it to become a new index loop.

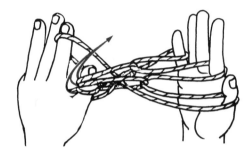

11. Turn your hands so that the fingers are pointing away from you. Two diagonal strings run up towards the right from the bottom framing string of the figure. One crosses the right little finger loop, and one hooks around the loop where the right far thumb string and the right near index string meet.

12. Your left thumb reaches over to go, from below, up into the right little finger loop. It catches these two strings and returns with them to its usual position.

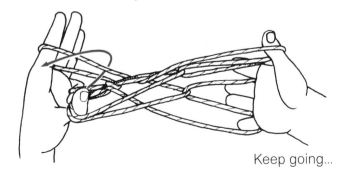

Keep going...

14. Use your teeth or fingers to Navaho the left thumb loops. The two lower loops go up over the upper loop and up over the top of your left thumb.

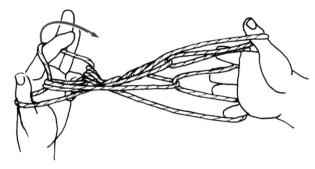

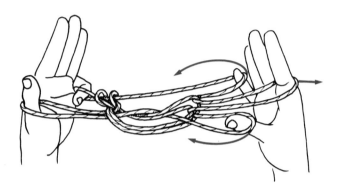

15. Your left index finger drops its loop.

16. Now drop the loops from your right thumb and little finger and pull the right index loop out as far as it will go.

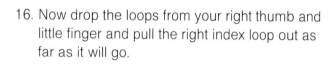

17. Your right middle, ring finger, and little finger go, from above, down into the right index loop. Your right index finger joins the other fingers of your right hand in their loop.

Here is the Inuit chant that goes with this figure:

A red fox with a long tail
Ran to a place where there was no wind,
Ran to a place where there was no wind,
Either around him
Or above him
mu-hu mu-hu
The fox's cry.

Diamond Jenness

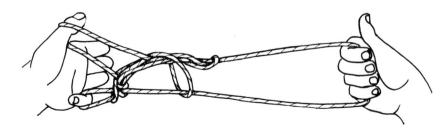

The Fastenings of the Raven's Plumage

This string game was collected from the Bella Coola Indians of British Columbia. Legend says that the first people floated down to earth as ravens. When they reached the ground, they took off their feathers and became human beings. As you pull the strings off your fingers, you show how easily the fastenings of each raven's plumage came undone, and how easy the transformation was from bird to human.

1. Hang the string loop on your left thumb. Your left hand is in the basic position.

2. Your right middle, ring, and little fingers hold both strings of the string loop about 15 cm (six inches) from your left thumb. Your right thumb and index finger go, from above, down into the left thumb loop.

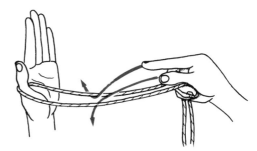

Keep your right thumb and index finger about five cm (two inches) apart and let the long loop slip through the fingers of your right hand as you weave the figure on the fingers of your left.

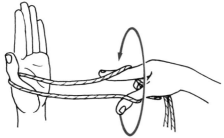

3. Rotate your right hand towards you until your right index finger and thumb are pointing up. There is an X in the left thumb loop.

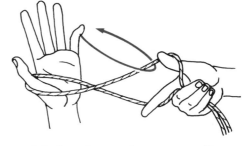

4. Your left little finger goes, from above, down into the right index/thumb space to the right of the X. It catches on its back the far right thumb string and returns.

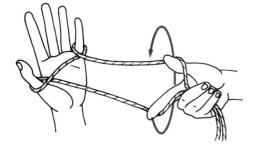

5. Rotate your right hand away from you until your right thumb and index finger once again point up. You have put a twist in the strings they are holding.

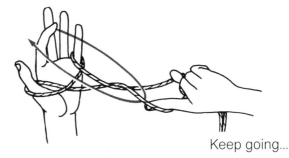

6. Your left index finger goes, from above, down into the right thumb/index space to the right of the twist. It catches on its back the near right index string and returns.

Keep going...

7. Rotate your right hand towards you until your right thumb and index finger are pointing up again. You have made an X in the strings they are holding.

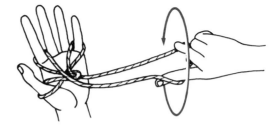

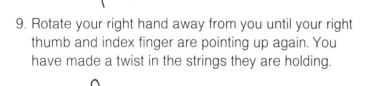

8. Your left ring finger goes, from above, down into the right thumb/index space to the right of the X. It catches on its back the right far thumb string and returns.

9. Rotate your right hand away from you until your right thumb and index finger are pointing up again. You have made a twist in the strings they are holding.

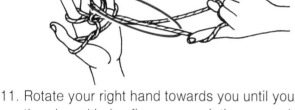

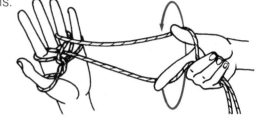

10. Your left middle finger goes, from above, down into the right thumb/index space to the right of the twist. It catches on its back the right near index string and returns.

11. Rotate your right hand towards you until your right thumb and index finger are pointing up again. There is an X in the strings they are holding.

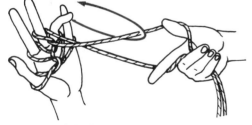

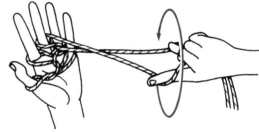

12. Your left ring finger goes, from below, up into the right thumb/index space to the right of the X. It catches on its back the right far thumb string and returns.

13. Rotate your right hand away from you until your right thumb and index finger are pointing up again. There is a twist in the strings they are holding.

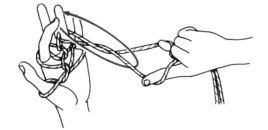

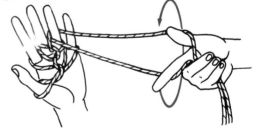

14. Your left index finger goes, from below, up into the right thumb/index space to the right of the twist. It catches on its back the right near index string and returns.

15. Rotate your right hand towards you until your right thumb and index finger are pointing up again. There is a twist in the strings they are holding.

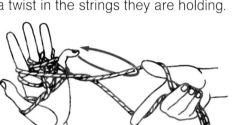

17. Rotate your right hand away from you until your right thumb and index finger are pointing up again. There is a twist in the strings they are holding.

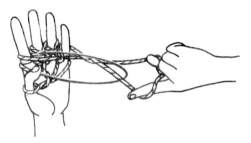

19. Your right hand has finished weaving the figure and can now let go of its strings. Your left thumb, index finger, ring finger, and little finger each have two loops. Your left middle finger has only one loop.

To show how easily the ravens were able to unfasten their plumage and become human beings, take the single loop off your left middle finger. Now begin to unravel the figure by pulling gently on the hanging strings. You may have to help things along a bit with your right hand. Don't pull too tightly or too quickly — the raven will become tangled in his plumage. And don't let the loops jump off their fingers before it is their turn, as this can also cause tangling.

If you can find a slippery string to use, the figure will come apart more easily.

Collected by T.F. McIlwraith

16. Your left little finger goes, from below, up into the right thumb/index space to the right of the twist. It catches on its back the right far thumb string and returns.

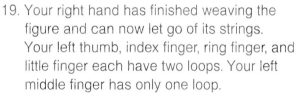

18. Your left thumb goes, from below, up into the right thumb/index space to the right of the twist. It catches on its back the right near index string and returns.

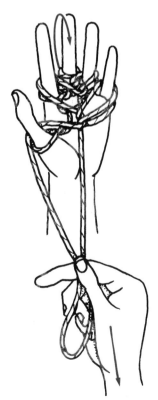

Fanene's Skipping Rope

Fanene's Skipping Rope comes from Tonga. When you've made the figure, you can make the long skipping rope loop flip backwards and forwards over the strings.

The Skipping Rope begins with the Murray Island Opening, with a twist.

1. Hold the string loop with your hands about 10 cm (four inches) apart.

2. Make a small loop in the string you are holding.

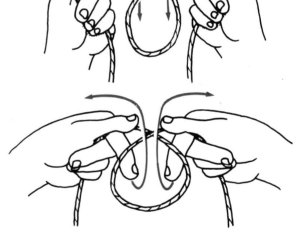

3. Put your index fingers, from behind, into this small string loop.
   Your index fingers are pointing towards you. The rest of your fingers are still holding the strings of the long hanging loop.

4. Turn your index fingers up and rotate your hands until they are facing each other.

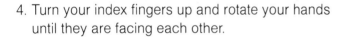

5. Your middle, ring, and little fingers release the strings of the long hanging loop and straighten up.
   Now pull your hands apart as far as they will go.
   Steps 1 to 5 make the Murray Opening.

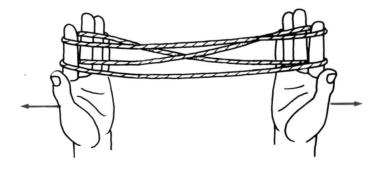

Each index finger has an upper and a lower loop. Be sure to keep these loops separate, and don't let them get mixed up.

The near index strings are straight strings which run from side to side across the figure. The far index strings make a string cross.

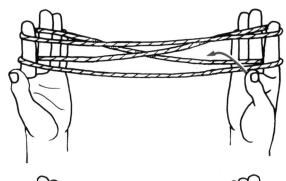

6. Now you want to put one twist in the upper right index loop only, so hook your right thumb down over both strings of the lower right index loop to hold them out of the way. Rotate your right index finger away from you, down, towards you, and up to twist the loop.

Your thumb releases the strings it is holding down and returns.

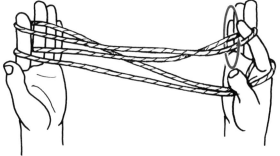

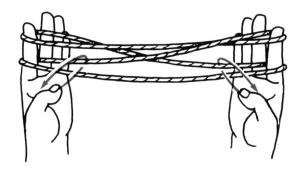

7. Your thumbs go over the lower near index string to get the lower far index strings and return.

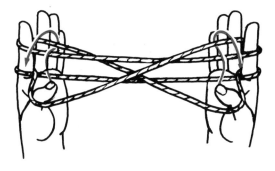

8. Your thumbs, without losing their loops, go over the upper near index strings to get the upper far index strings and return.

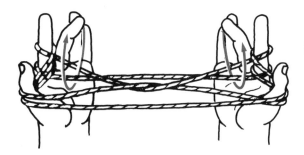

9. Turn your hands so that the palms are facing you. Your middle fingers hook down over the upper near index strings. They pick up the lower near index string on their backs and return.

10. The upper near index string crosses the front of each middle finger.

Each middle finger also has a far string. These strings are twisted around each other. You want to twist them around each other several more times so . . .

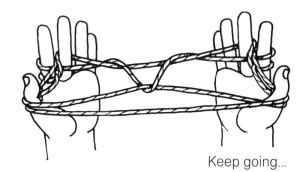

Keep going...

11. Your teeth pick up the string which crosses the front of your left middle finger.

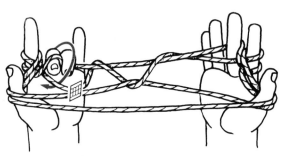

Your Teeth

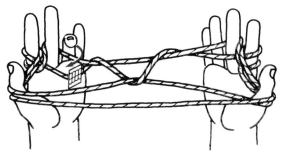

12. Your left ring finger hooks down over, and holds, the far left middle finger string.

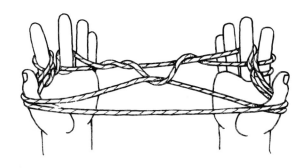

13. Now take your middle finger out of its space and put it back into its space from above. Let go of the string you are holding in your mouth.

14. Your left ring finger releases the left far middle finger string and returns.
Your left middle finger straightens up carrying the old mouth string on its back. You have put one more twist in the strings around your left middle finger.

Repeat steps 11, 12, 13, and 14 twice more to put two more twists in the strings around your left middle finger.

To put extra twists in the strings around your right middle finger . . .

15. Your teeth pick up the string which crosses the front of your right middle finger.

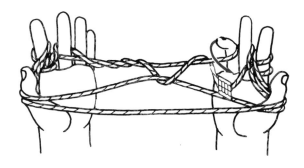

16. Your right ring finger hooks down over, and holds, the far right middle finger string.

17. Take your right middle finger out of its space and put it back into its space from above. Let go of the string you are holding in your mouth.

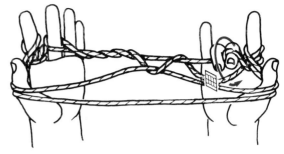

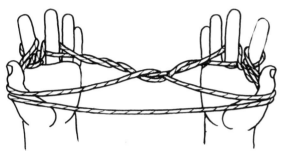

18. Your right ring finger releases the right far middle finger string and returns.
Your right middle finger straightens up carrying the old mouth string on its back. You have put one more twist in the strings around your right middle finger.

Repeat steps 15, 16, 17, and 18 twice more to put two more twists in the strings around your right middle finger.

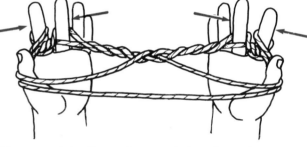

19. Return your hands to the basic position and press each index finger and middle finger together to stop the strings between them from slipping.

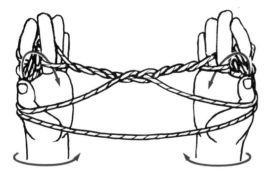

20. To extend the figure by untwisting the strings you have just twisted, your thumbs hook over and press down on the strings which cross the fronts of your middle fingers. As you press down on these strings, turn your hands so that the palms are facing away from you.

You will see that there is one long loop, the skipping rope, hanging free at the front of the figure. You can flip the skipping rope backwards and forwards over the top of the extended figure.

To take the skipping rope apart, just drop the loops from your thumbs and middle fingers and pull your hands apart to tighten the strings.
You are back to the end of step 6, so you can practise the figure again if you like!

Collected by James Hornell

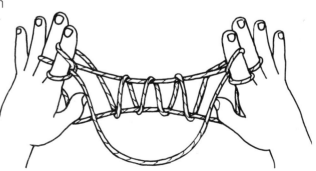

The Kayak

This string figure of an Inuit hunting boat was first recorded by Dr. G.B. Gordon in 1906. There are several ways of making it, but I find this the easiest. You can make this three-dimensional string figure dissolve — or capsize — by simply dropping a couple of loops and Navahoing.

1. Do Opening A.

2. Your thumbs go under the strings of the index loops. They get the far index strings and return under the near index strings.

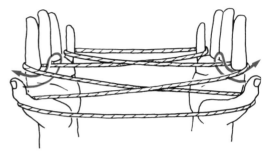

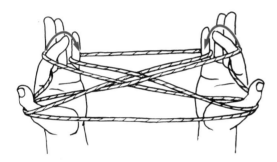

3. Your index fingers drop their loops. Each thumb now has two loops. Be sure to keep them apart and don't let them get mixed up.

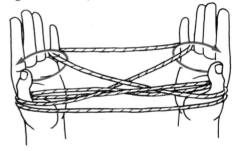

4. Your thumbs, carrying their double loops go, from below, up into the little finger loops to get the near little finger strings and return.

5. Your little fingers drop their loops. You've transferred the little finger loops to your thumbs.

Each thumb now has three loops. Try to keep them apart and don't let them get mixed up. The loop with the near straight string which runs across the figure from side to side must always be the lowest of the three.

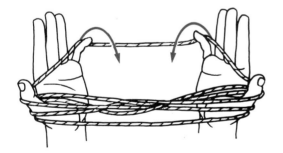

6. Turn your hands so that the palms are facing you. Now your little fingers can come towards you to go up into the thumb loops. They get the two lower far thumb strings and return. The far string they leave must be a straight string which runs across the figure from side to side.

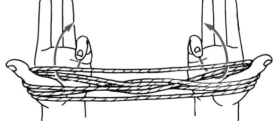

7. Your little fingers come towards you again to go, from above, down into the thumb loops. They hook down over the upper straight far thumb string. The little finger loops are now held in the hooks of your little fingers. Don't worry about the old little finger loops.

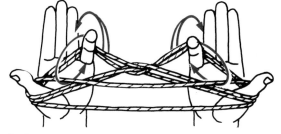

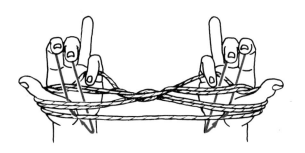

8. Your index fingers and middle fingers tip down, from above, into the thumb loops.
   Your index fingers come out towards you through the space between the lowest and middle near thumb strings.
   Your middle fingers come towards you under the lowest near thumb string. Now pinch the lowest near thumb string — a straight string — between your index and middle fingers.

9. Turn your hands until the palms are facing away from you and straighten up your index fingers. The lowest near thumb string curves around your index fingers to become the new index loops.

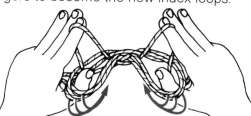

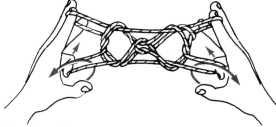

10. Your thumbs drop all their loops. Turn your hands so that the fingers are pointing away from you.

11. Your thumbs go, from behind, into the little finger loops. They take the loops from your little fingers. Your little fingers drop their loops.

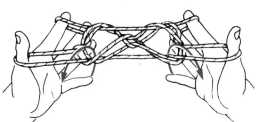

Now you are going to *Katilluik* the thumb loops. Katilluik is an Inuit word which means "put two things together."
You are going to put the thumb loops together, so:

13. Your right thumb goes, from below, up into the left thumb loop.

14. Your left thumb drops its loop.

12. Double straight strings cross each thumb loop. Your little fingers come towards you to hook over these double strings. Continue to hold these strings in the hooks of your little fingers.

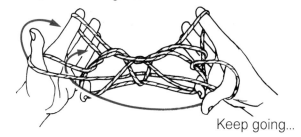

Keep going...

15. Your left thumb goes, from below, up into both right thumb loops and returns.

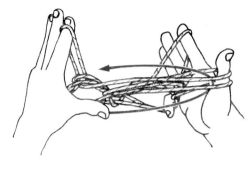

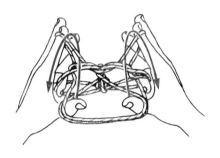

16. Your thumbs, without losing their loops, go from below, up into the index loops and return with the near index strings.

17. Now Navaho the thumb loops. The lower double thumb loops go up over the single upper thumb loops and up over the tops of your thumbs.

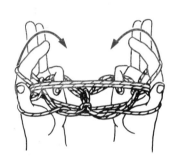

18. Your index fingers drop their loops. The "putting together" is finished.

The Kayak is upside down. To turn it the right way up without putting it down on your lap:

19. Turn your hands until the palms are facing each other again. Your index fingers go, from above, down into the loops held in the hooks of your little fingers. They get the double far little finger strings (use your middle fingers to help out) and return.
As they do this, your little fingers drop their loops.

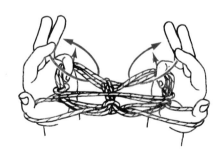

20. Turn your hands so that the palms are facing you. Your little fingers come towards you to go, from below, up into the thumb loops.
They hook down over the near thumb string as your thumbs drop their loops.

21. Each index finger has two loops. The near index strings are straight strings. Each straight string has a little loop over it. You want to separate these loops so that you can see the hole in the centre of the kayak where the hunter sits.

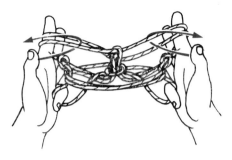

If you turn your hands so that the fingers are facing away from you, you will see that one of these straight strings, with its little loop, is nearer to you than the other. Your thumbs get this straight string.

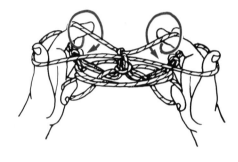

22. Your index fingers gently drop their loops. Put your index fingers back into the empty index loops from the opposite direction — from the back.

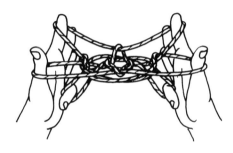

This is the Kayak, a beautiful three-dimensional figure which can be admired from all angles.

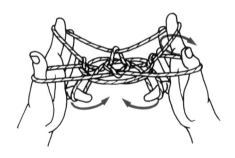

To make the Kayak capsize:
Your little fingers drop their loops.

Your right thumb goes, from below, up into the right index loop and returns with the near index string.

Navaho the right thumb loop.

Your right index finger drops its loop.

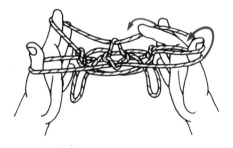

Now pull your hands apart and watch this complicated figure simply evaporate!

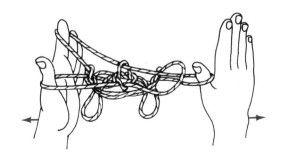

The Salmon River

This Tlingit Indian string story follows the course of the Salmon River as it flows between two mountains, past a range of mountains, then down to the plain where it flows past only one mountain. Along the way we meet a mosquito and a fisherman who really casts his line to catch his fish!

1. Do Opening A.

2. Your thumbs go under the near index strings to get the far index strings. They return under the near index strings.

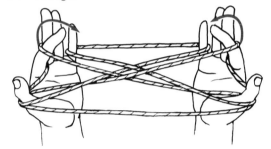

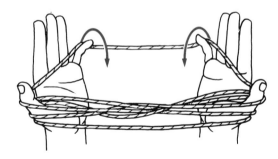

3. Your index fingers drop their loops.
   Each thumb now has two loops. Be sure to keep them apart and don't let them get mixed up.

4. Your thumbs, carrying their double loops go, from below, up into the little finger loops.
   They get the near little finger strings and return.

5. Your little fingers drop their loops.

   Each thumb now has three loops. Keep these loops apart and don't let them change places. Make sure that the lowest near thumb string is a straight string.

6. Turn your hands so that the palms are facing you. Your little fingers go, from below, up into the thumb loops.
   Each little finger catches on its back the two lower far thumb strings and pushes them away from you out under the upper far thumb string.

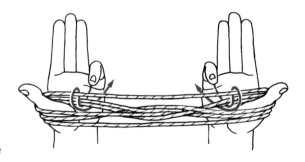

7. Now your little fingers hook down over, and hold, the upper far thumb string.

8. Your right index finger goes down into the upper right thumb loop. It comes out towards you between the upper right near thumb string and the middle right near thumb string.

   Now your right index finger can catch on its back the right upper near thumb string.

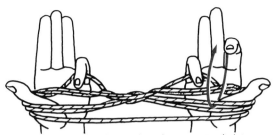

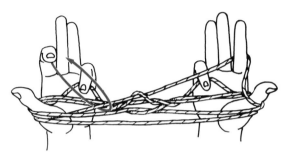

9. As your right index finger begins to straighten up, carrying the upper near thumb string on its back, you will see that the new right far index string is a straight string with a mountain looped over it.

10. Now your left index finger tips down and goes under the straight string carrying the mountain. It catches this straight string on its back and straightens up. Now the far index string, carrying the mountain, runs across the figure from index finger to index finger.

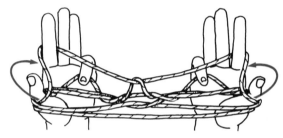

11. Your thumbs release only the loops whose near string has been taken by the index fingers.
    Each thumb still has two loops.
    The lower near thumb string must be a straight string which runs across the figure from thumb to thumb. This string is the river.

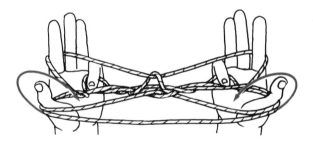

To make the river flowing past the range of mountains:

12. Use your fingers or teeth to Navaho the thumb loops. When you hold the figure with your fingers pointing away from you, you can see the Salmon River — the straight string in the middle — flowing along between two mountains.
    Keep your eyes on the river.

13. Your middle fingers go, from below, up into the index loops. They go over the river and down into the thumb loops. Then they come out towards you under the near thumb string.

    Your index fingers tip down out of their loops over the near thumb string.

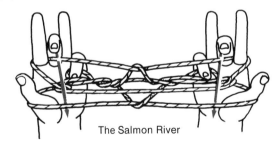

The Salmon River

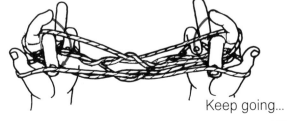

Keep going...

59

14. Your index fingers and middle fingers pinch the near thumb string between them.

Now turn your hands until the palms are facing away from you. Don't worry about the old index loops.

As your index fingers straighten up, the near thumb string will curve around them to become new index loops.

15. Your thumbs drop their loops.

Turn your hands so that the fingers are pointing away from you.

Now you can see the river — the straight string — flowing past a whole range of mountains.

To make the Mosquito that lives on the river:

16. Your thumbs go away from you over the river string. They catch on their backs the strings which cross the index loops and return.

The mosquito's sharp proboscis is looped around the near thumb string.

The wings are made by the river string and the double strings which cross the little finger loops.

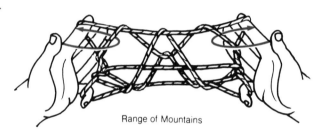

Range of Mountains

To show the river flowing across the plains, past just one mountain:

17. Your index fingers drop their loops.

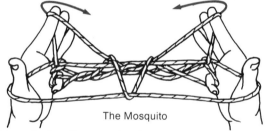

The Mosquito

18. Your index fingers tip down to go, from above, into the thumb loops. They come out towards you under the near thumb string.

19. Your index fingers catch the near thumb string on their backs and straighten up to return to their position. Keep these new index loops high up on your index fingers.

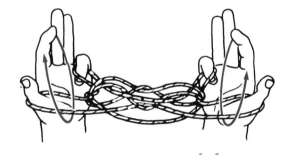

20. Your thumbs drop their loops.

Pull your hands apart to tighten the strings of the figure.

You should still be able to see the straight river string running across the figure from side to side.

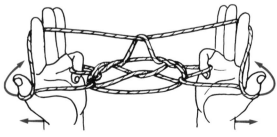

To make the fisherman standing up in his boat and his salmon:

21. Your left thumb goes up behind the river string and returns carrying this string on its back.

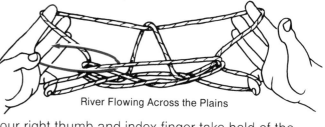

River Flowing Across the Plains

22. Your right thumb and index finger take hold of the left near thumb string and wrap this string once around your left thumb.
Don't lose the right index loop as you do this.

23. Now your right thumb goes, from below, up into the two left thumb loops and returns. Each thumb now has two loops.

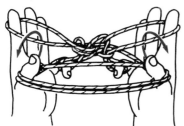

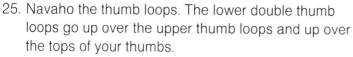

24. Your thumbs go, from below, up into the index loops and return carrying the near index strings.

25. Navaho the thumb loops. The lower double thumb loops go up over the upper thumb loops and up over the tops of your thumbs.

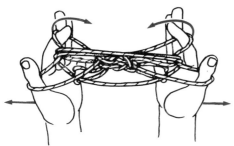

26. Your index fingers drop their loops. Keep the thumb loops high up on your thumbs and pull your hands apart to extend the figure.

Now you can see the fisherman standing up in his boat on the left, and the salmon he wants to catch on the right.

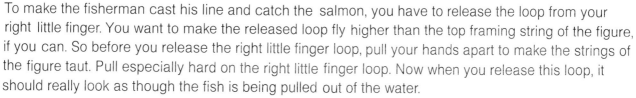

The Fisherman

To make the fisherman cast his line and catch the salmon, you have to release the loop from your right little finger. You want to make the released loop fly higher than the top framing string of the figure, if you can. So before you release the right little finger loop, pull your hands apart to make the strings of the figure taut. Pull especially hard on the right little finger loop. Now when you release this loop, it should really look as though the fish is being pulled out of the water.

Collected by Dr. G.B. Gordon

61

Four Stars of Itai Leaves and Their Well

Many of the classic string figures from the South Pacific are woven with a very long string. Four Stars of Itai Leaves and Their Well comes from the Gilbert Islands, coral islands where water is scarce and there are periods of drought. Because of this, diamond shapes in string figures often represent wells, symbols of beauty and fruitfulness. I like this figure because of its logical construction and its magical Caroline Extension. Use your long string for this figure.

1. Do Opening A, but pick up the right palmar string first. Put a twist in each loop of the opening.

2. To twist the little finger loops away from you, use your opposite index finger and thumb to take hold of both strings of each little finger loop. Rotate each little finger away from you, down, towards you under both little finger strings, and up. Your index finger and thumb let go of their strings.

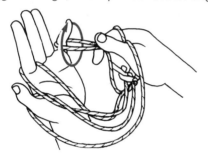 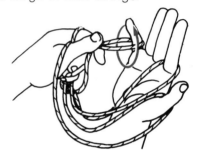

3. Repeat this to put a twist away from you in each index finger loop. Once again, the fingers are rotated away from you, down, towards you under both strings of the loop, and up.

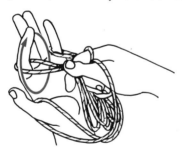 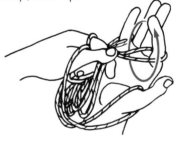

4. The thumb loops are twisted towards you. Take hold of the strings of each thumb loop and rotate each thumb towards you, down, then away from you under the strings of the loop, and up.

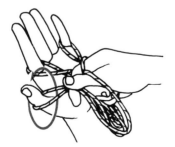 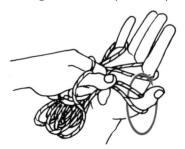

Now begin to weave the figure.

5. Your thumbs go over the strings of the index loops to get the near little finger strings and return.

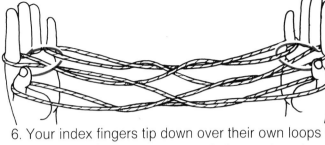

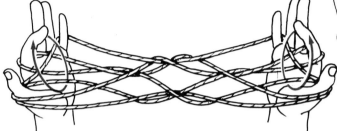

6. Your index fingers tip down over their own loops and the palmar strings to go, from below, up into the thumb loops. They get the far thumb strings and return.

7. Your thumbs drop both their loops.

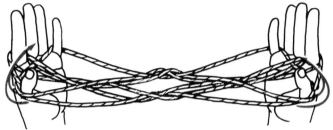

8. Your thumbs go, from below, up into the upper index loops. They get the upper near index strings and return.

9. Your index fingers drop their upper loops. You have transferred the upper index loops to your thumbs.

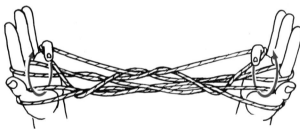

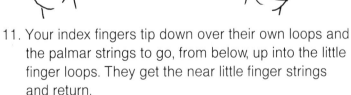

10. Your little fingers come towards you over the index loops to get the far thumb strings and return.

11. Your index fingers tip down over their own loops and the palmar strings to go, from below, up into the little finger loops. They get the near little finger strings and return.

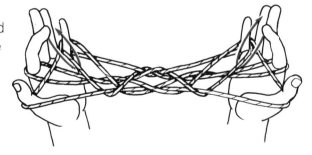

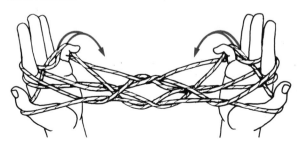

12. Your little fingers drop both their loops.

Keep going...

13. Your little fingers go, from below, up into the upper index loops. They get the upper far index strings and return.

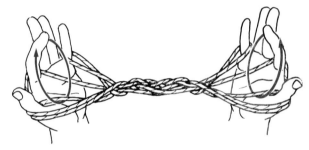

15. Your thumbs go, from below, up into the index loops. They get the near index strings and return.

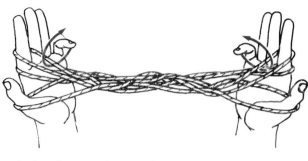

14. Your index fingers drop their upper loops. You have transferred the upper index loops to your little fingers.

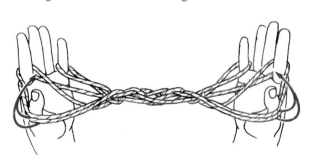

17. Your thumbs drop both their loops.

16. Your index fingers, without losing their loops, tip down to get the far thumb strings and return.

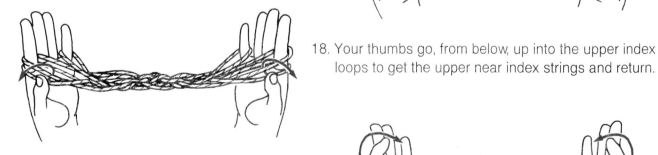

19. Your index fingers drop their upper loops. You've transferred the upper index loops to your thumbs.

18. Your thumbs go, from below, up into the upper index loops to get the upper near index strings and return.

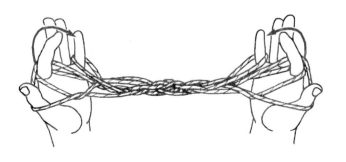

20. Your little fingers go, from below, up into the index loops to get the far index strings and return.

22. Your little fingers drop both their loops.

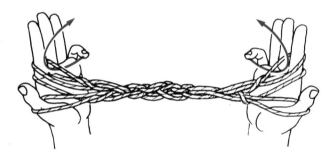

24. Your index fingers drop their upper loops. You've transferred the upper index loops to your little fingers.

26. Your index fingers tip down to go, from above, into the thumb loops. They get the near thumb strings and return. Let your thumbs slip out of their loops.

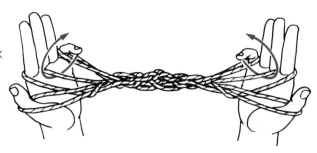

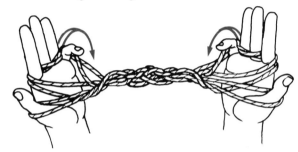

21. Your index fingers, without losing their loops, go from below, up into the little finger loops. They get the near little finger strings and return.

23. Your little fingers go, from below, up into the upper index loops to get the upper far index strings and return.

25. Your index fingers drop their remaining loops. Pull your hands apart a little.

Keep going...

27. Your thumbs go under the strings of the index loops to get the near little finger strings. As they return, they go up into the index loops and also bring back the near index strings.

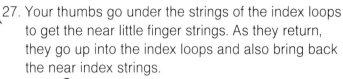

28. Your index fingers drop their loops.

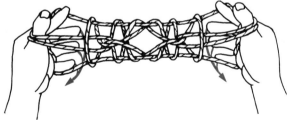

30. Your thumbs press against the strings which run from your index fingers down to your thumbs. Keep each index finger and thumb, with the string between them, pressed tightly together. Don't let this string move at all.

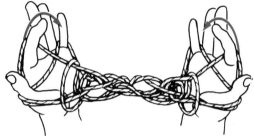

Now to do that magical Caroline Extension:

29. Turn your hands until the palms are facing up. Your index fingers tip down over the palmar strings. They go, from below, up into the thumb loops and return with the far thumb strings. Keep these strings high up on your index fingers.

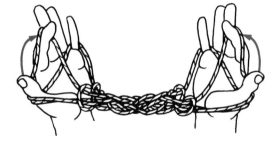

31. Now turn your hands so that the palms are facing out. Keep your index fingers tall, but curl your middle, ring, and little fingers down over the far little finger string.

Two leaves are looped around the framing strings on each side of the central diamond well.

To make the Four Leaves without the well, follow steps 1 to 31, but leave out steps 2, 3, and 4 because the pattern is made without putting twists in the string loops of Opening A.

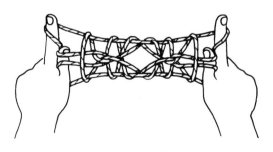

Collected by Honor Maude

66

Little Fishes

This figure appears all over the South Pacific. Sometimes, it's simply called W, but it's also known as Little Fishes, Dancing Sunbeams (its Hawaiian name), and a piece of wood for knocking down coconuts.

By putting an extra twist in the opening strings, you can fool your friends into thinking you've made a mistake. Only you know how to untwist the strings to show them that the figure was there all the time.

When you've made the four little fishes, you can go on to make the wonderful walking Porker, or pig.

Little Fishes begins with the Murray Island Opening.

1. Hold the string loop with your hands about 10 cm (four inches) apart.

2. Make a small loop in the string you are holding.

3. Put your index fingers from behind into this small string loop. Your index fingers are pointing towards you. The rest of your fingers are still holding the strings of the long hanging loop.

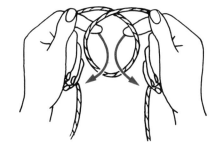

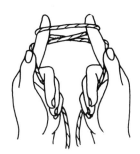

4. Turn your index fingers up and rotate your hands until they are facing each other.

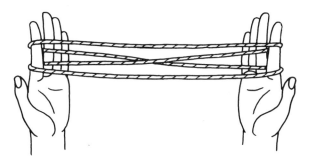

5. Your middle, ring, and little fingers release the strings of the long hanging loop and straighten up. Now pull your hands apart as far as they will go. This is the Murray Opening.

Each index finger has an upper and a lower loop. Be sure to keep these loops separate and don't let them get mixed up. The near index strings are straight strings which run from side to side across the figure. The far index strings make a string cross.

6. Your thumbs go over the lower near index string to get the lower far index strings and return.

Keep going...

7. Your thumbs, without losing their loops, go over the upper near index string to get the upper far index strings and return.

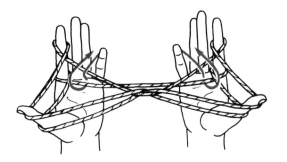

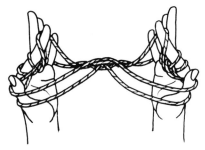

8. Turn your hands so that the palms are facing you. Your little fingers come towards you and hook down over the upper near index strings.

9. Your little fingers carry these strings away from you, then they go under the lower near index string and return to their usual position carrying this string on their backs. Don't worry about the strings you were holding in the hooks of your little fingers.

10. A straight string crosses each little finger loop. Turn your hands until the palms are facing away from you. Now your index fingers can tip down into the little finger loops and hook down over these straight strings.

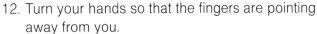

11. Turn your hands so that the palms are facing you. When you straighten up your index fingers, you will see that these straight strings have curved around your index fingers to become new index loops. Each index finger now has three loops.

12. Turn your hands so that the fingers are pointing away from you.
Your thumbs drop their double loops.
Now you can see the four little fishes chasing each other around the framing strings of the figure, or the four sunbeams dancing around the strings.

If you like, you can keep the strings on your fingers and go on to make the continuation of Little Fishes, the Porker.

To undo Little Fishes, your index fingers drop their upper loops (the ones near the tip of your index fingers), then your little fingers drop their loops. You've returned to the Murray Opening.

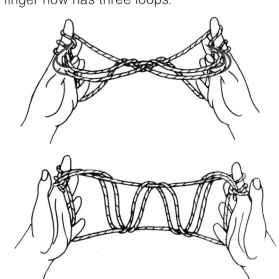

A Trick

In Papua New Guinea, expert string game players used this figure with an extra twist to fool people into thinking they had made a mistake. Of course, it's not a mistake, but a trick to show everyone how skillful you are in making the figure appear out of a tangle of strings.

Tell everyone you are going to make Little Fishes.

1. Do the Murray Opening, steps 1-5 of Little Fishes.

2. Now put a twist in the strings of both left index loops. Rotate your left index finger away from you, down, towards you, and up. Be careful that the index loops don't get mixed up as you do this. Keep each one in its place and keep them apart. If you are in the company of expert string players, try to distract them so they won't notice this extra move.

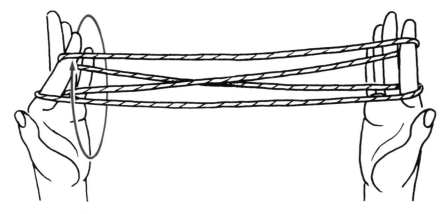

3. Now continue to make Little Fishes as usual, steps 6-12.

   This time, when you drop the double thumb loops, you cannot make the Little Fishes flash into view. This is because the framing strings are tangled around each other.

4. To make Little Fishes, you must untwist the framing strings. Look carefully at the twist. You will have to rotate your whole right hand to undo it.

   When you are finished, you are holding the figure awkwardly, but your friends will be amazed when Little Fishes appears.

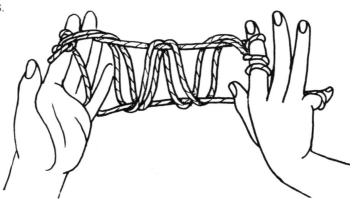

Collected by A.C. Haddon

The Porker/The Pig

This wonderful walking Porker, or pig, was first collected from Lifu in the Loyalty Islands of the South Pacific. The method described here is a little different from the traditional way of making the figure, but the end result is the same.

Don't forget to say, "Down she goes," and "Come along, Porker," at the right times.

1. Make Little Fishes.

2. Your thumbs go into the little finger loops. They get, from behind, the double strings which make the sides of the W and return.

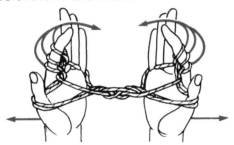

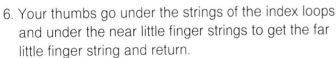

3. Return your hands to the basic position. Your index fingers drop all their loops. Use your opposite index finger and thumb to slide the loops off. Pull your hands apart as far as they will go.

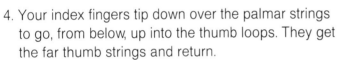

4. Your index fingers tip down over the palmar strings to go, from below, up into the thumb loops. They get the far thumb strings and return.

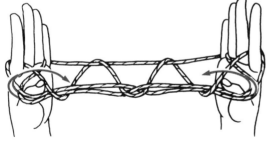

5. Your thumbs drop both their loops.

6. Your thumbs go under the strings of the index loops and under the near little finger strings to get the far little finger string and return.

7. Your little fingers drop their loops.

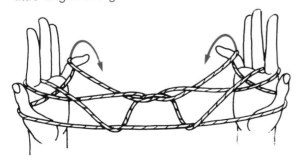

8. Your little fingers come towards you under the strings of the index loops to get the far thumb strings. If you pinch the far thumb strings between your little and ring fingers, it's easier to carry them back under the strings of the index loops.

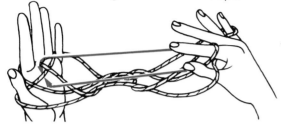

Continue to hold the palmar string while your left thumb and little finger drop their loops.

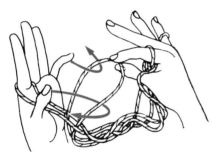

11. Your left thumb and index finger reach through the right index loop to take hold of the right palmar string.

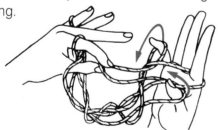

12. Pull the right palmar string out through the right index loop, then put it back on your right hand in Position 1. Now the right palmar string runs over the right index loop.

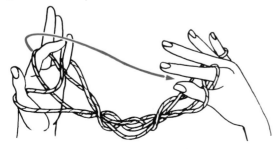

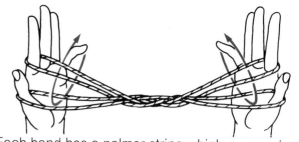

9. Each hand has a palmar string which runs under the index loop.
Your right thumb and index finger reach through the left index loop to take hold of the left palmar string.

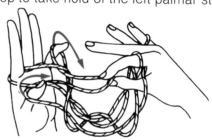

10. Pull the left palmar string out through the left index loop and then put it back on your left hand in Position 1. Now the left palmar string runs over the left index loop.

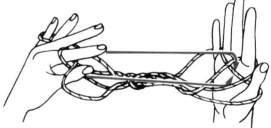

They continue to hold the palmar string while your right thumb and little finger drop their loops.

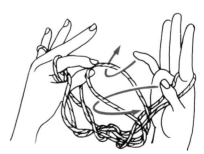

13. Your right thumb and index finger take the loop off your left index finger.

Keep going...

Put the fingers and thumb of your left hand together and slip your whole left hand through the left index loop. As you do this say, "Down she goes."

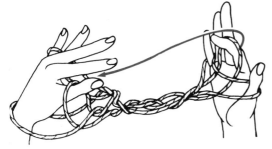

Put the fingers and thumb of your right hand together and slip your whole right hand through the right index loop. Say, "Down she goes."

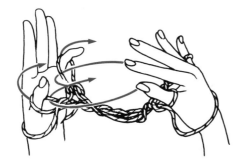

16. Slip your left hand out of its wrist loop and put your left thumb and little finger back into their loops.

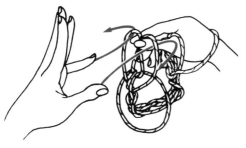

17. Your left thumb and index finger take hold of the right far thumb string and the right near little finger string.
They continue to hold these strings while your right thumb and little finger drop their loops.

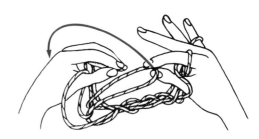

14. Your left thumb and index finger take the loop off your right index finger.

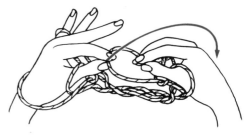

15. Your right thumb and index finger take hold of the left far thumb string and the left near little finger string.
They continue to hold these strings while your left thumb and little finger drop their loops.

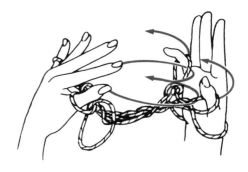

Your right thumb and index finger drop the strings they were holding.

18. Slip your right hand out of its wrist loop and put your right thumb and little finger back into their loops. Your left thumb and index finger drop the strings they were holding.
Hold the figure gently. Don't pull your hands apart yet.

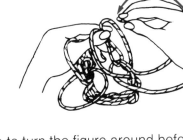

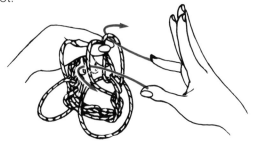

You have to turn the figure around before you can extend it, so you'll have to shift the loops around on your fingers.

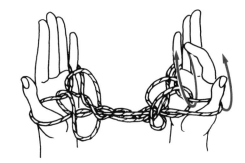

19. Your right index finger tips down to go, from below, up into the right thumb loop. Your right thumb drops its loop.

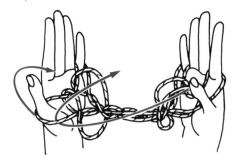

20. Your right thumb goes, from below, up into the left thumb loop. Your left thumb drops its loop.

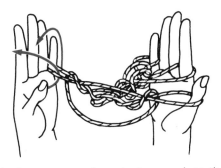

21. Your left thumb goes, from below, up into the left little finger loop. Your left little finger drops its loop.

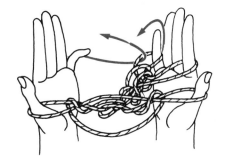

22. Your left little finger goes, from below, up into the right little finger loop. Your right little finger drops its loop.

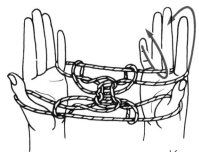

23. Your right little finger goes, from below, up into the right index loop. Your right index finger drops its loop.

Keep going...

24. The figure is now held on thumbs and little fingers. Pull your hands apart. You will see the Porker spread-eagled across the strings.

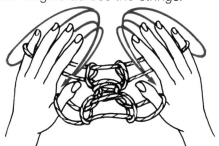

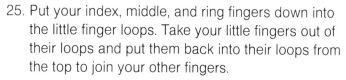

To make the Porker stand up:

25. Put your index, middle, and ring fingers down into the little finger loops. Take your little fingers out of their loops and put them back into their loops from the top to join your other fingers.

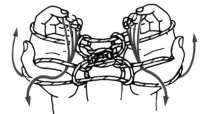

26. Your index, middle, ring, and little fingers go, from below up into the thumb loops and hook down over the near thumb string.

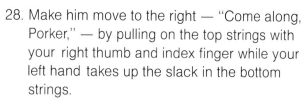

27. Your thumbs drop their loops.

Now the fat, four-legged Porker can walk along the string.

28. Make him move to the right — "Come along, Porker," — by pulling on the top strings with your right thumb and index finger while your left hand takes up the slack in the bottom strings.

29. To make him walk the other way, pull on the top strings of the figure with your left thumb and index finger while your right hand takes up the slack in the bottom strings. Say, "Porker, go away."

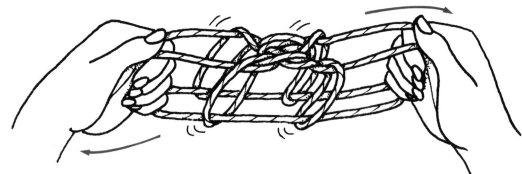

To undo the Porker, first find the four strings which make up his body. Now pull the two outside strings apart until the whole figure dissolves.

Collected by R.H. Compton

74

The Frog

I love this Frog, from his googly eyes down to his rather large feet. He was probably discovered by someone trying to remember how to make the Porker, because all the moves except one are identical.

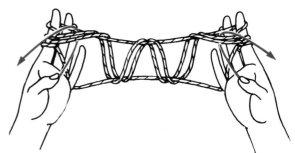

1. To make the Frog, first make Little Fishes and return your hands to the basic position.

2. Here is the move that is different from the Porker. Your thumbs go, from below, to get the double strings of the W which loop over the top far index string and return.

Now follow the steps of the Porker, 3 to 24.

This time, when you pull your hands apart, the figure is finished. You can make the eyes bigger by pulling the eye loops farther up on their strings.

To show off your frog, turn your hands so that the fingers are pointing away from you, then move your left hand up and your right hand down until the figure is vertical.

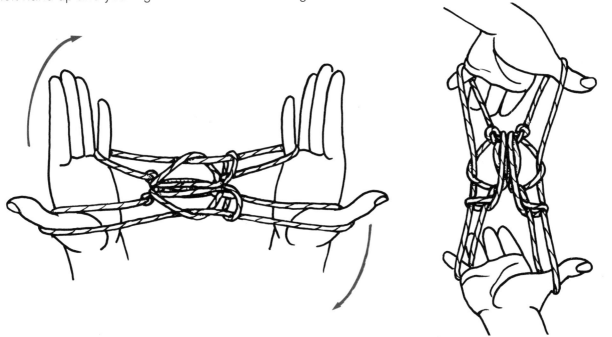

To take the Frog apart, first return your hands to the basic position. Now follow the far thumb strings into the diamond-shaped body of the frog. Find the loops made by these strings as they curve around the other strings of the figure. Now pick up these loops inside the diamond body of the frog and pull them apart. The figure will dissolve without a knot.

The Little Dog with Big Ears

My favorite string figure was created by an unknown Inuit string artist and collected by Diamond Jenness. The Dog is a delight to make and is guaranteed to impress your friends.

1. Hang the string loop over the backs of your thumbs. Your thumbs are about 10 cm (four inches) apart. Your index fingers are pointing away from you and your middle, ring, and little fingers are holding the strings which cross your palms.

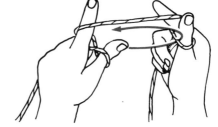

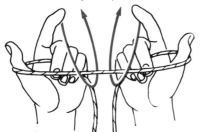

2. Turn your hands until the palms are facing up. Your index fingers hook towards you down over the near thumb string.
   Now turn your hands away from you until the palms are facing out and straighten up your index fingers. The near thumb string now curves around your index fingers.

Your hands are still facing each other about 10 cm (four inches) apart. Your thumbs are pointing up; your index fingers are pointing away from you. Your other fingers continue to hold the hanging strings.

3. Your left thumb goes, from below, up into the right thumb loop. It returns to its position carrying the straight string which runs between the right index finger and thumb.

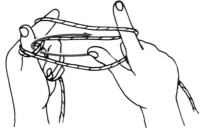

4. Your right thumb goes, from below, up into the left thumb loop. It returns to its position carrying the string which runs between the left index finger and thumb.

5. Your middle, ring, and little fingers let go of the strings they are holding and straighten up. Tighten the strings of the figure by pulling your hands apart as far as they will go.

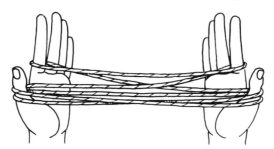

On your hands there are the following strings:
A near index string which runs from index finger to index finger; far index strings which cross and then run down to the thumbs to become far thumb strings. (N.B. The far right index string must cross over the *top* of the far left index string.) In addition to the far index/far thumb strings which form the cross, each thumb has a straight far thumb string which runs from thumb to thumb, and two straight near thumb strings.

6. Turn your hands so that the palms are facing you. Your little fingers come towards you under all the strings. They get the far straight thumb string and carry it, on their backs, out under all the strings.

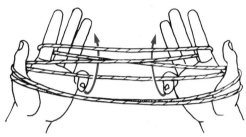

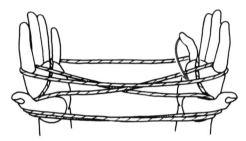

7. Now your right little finger hooks down over the right far index string (the top string of the cross). Don't worry about the string around your right little finger; it will look after itself.

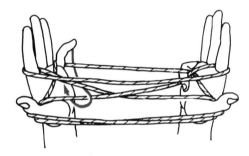

8. Your left little finger travels under the strings of the left index loop and hooks down over the left far thumb string. Don't worry about the string around your left little finger. Your little fingers are hooked down over the same straight string.
Return your hands to the basic position.

9. Each thumb has a true thumb loop with a near and a far string, and also a loop with a near straight string, and a far string that goes across your palms. The figure is not symmetrical.
To keep the true thumb loops but to get rid of the other thumb loops, hook your thumbs down over the far thumb strings and turn your hands so that the palms are facing out.
Your thumbs will keep their true loops, but the other thumb strings will slip off.

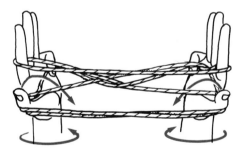

Straighten up your thumbs and return your hands to the basic position.

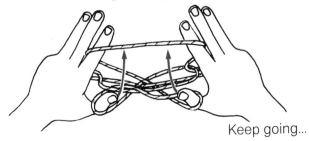

Keep going...

10. You now have thumb loops, index loops, and loops held in the hooks of your little fingers. There is an elaborate criss-cross arrangement in the middle of the figure. Your thumbs go up into the index loops and return to their position carrying the near index string.

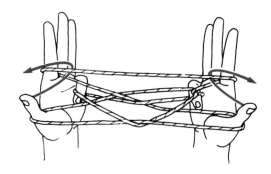

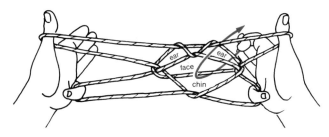

11. Navaho the thumb loops. Your index fingers release their loops.

12. Hold your hands with the fingers pointing away from you. You have actually made the head of the dog: two large ear triangles which are hooked over the near thumb string at the top of the figure; a chin triangle which runs under the straight little finger string at the bottom of the figure; and a flat string triangle which runs across the face just below the ear triangles.

13. Your right index finger comes from behind into the chin triangle. It catches like a hook the two strings of the flat face string triangle. (These strings do not hook over either of the straight framing strings of the figure.) Pull these strings back, up, and then stuff them towards you through the right thumb loop. Your right index finger has two strings on one side and one on the other. These strings will make a space in the next step.
Your right index finger is not actually holding any strings.

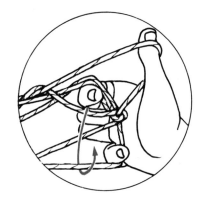

14. Your right index finger goes down in front of the other strings, then behind the straight bottom string of the figure. This string runs from little finger to little finger. Your right index finger catches this straight string in its hook, then carries it back out through the space made by the strings which were originally on each side of the index finger.

15. Your right index finger is now holding a loop.

Stuff your right index finger with its loop down through the right thumb loop. Your index finger is now at the front of the figure.

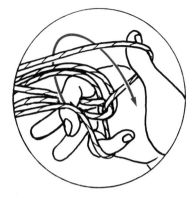

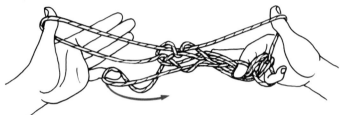

16. Your left little finger drops its loop. Your left thumb, with its loop, points up; your left fingers point to the right; you can see your left palm.

17. Your left hand travels in this position across the front of the figure. Your left little finger takes the loop from your right index finger and returns to its position. Your hands are pointing away from you. Your middle, ring, and little fingers are curled. Your thumbs, with their loops, are pointing up, and there are loops held in the hooks of your little fingers.

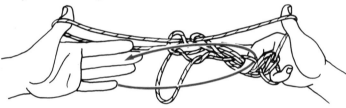

18. Now you must separate the dog's tail and back leg.
Your right index finger comes towards you through the big right thumb loop. Your right index finger starts to push back into the right little finger loop. The strings which make up the dog's tail and leg are being pushed away from you a little on the back of your index finger.

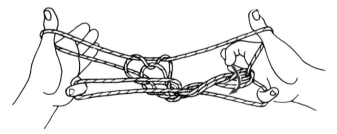

19. Your index finger can now go, from behind, up into the body of the dog and slide over the top of the double straight strings which make its back.

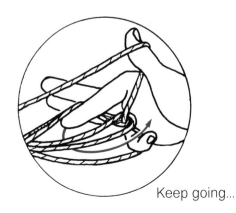

Keep going...

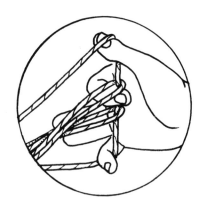

20. Your index finger then pulls back like a trigger, right back to the straight framing string which runs between your right thumb and little finger. You've split the loops which will make the tail and the leg.

21. To let the tail loop go up, take your right thumb out of its loop. Pull a bit with your right index finger and the tail loop will slide up. Put your right thumb back into its loop.

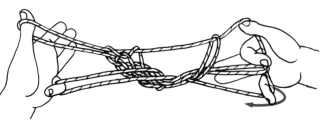

22. To let the leg loop go down, take your right little finger out of its loop. Pull a bit with your right index finger, and the leg loop will slide down.

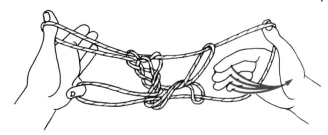

23. Now put all the fingers of your right hand down into the thumb loop. Your thumb should be pointing up to give the loop extra height.

Now the dog can walk along the string. Just pull gently with your right hand and the dog will travel. You can pull him back and let him walk across the string again.

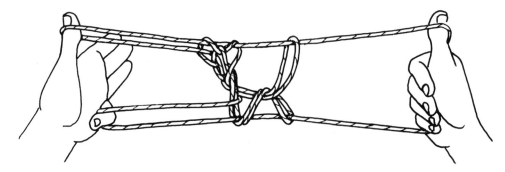

To take apart the Little Dog with Big Ears, just put your left index finger, from behind, into the dog's right ear loop. Now drop the loops from your left thumb and left little finger and pull out the ear loop as far as it will go.